DRAW 50
ENDANGERED
ANIMALS

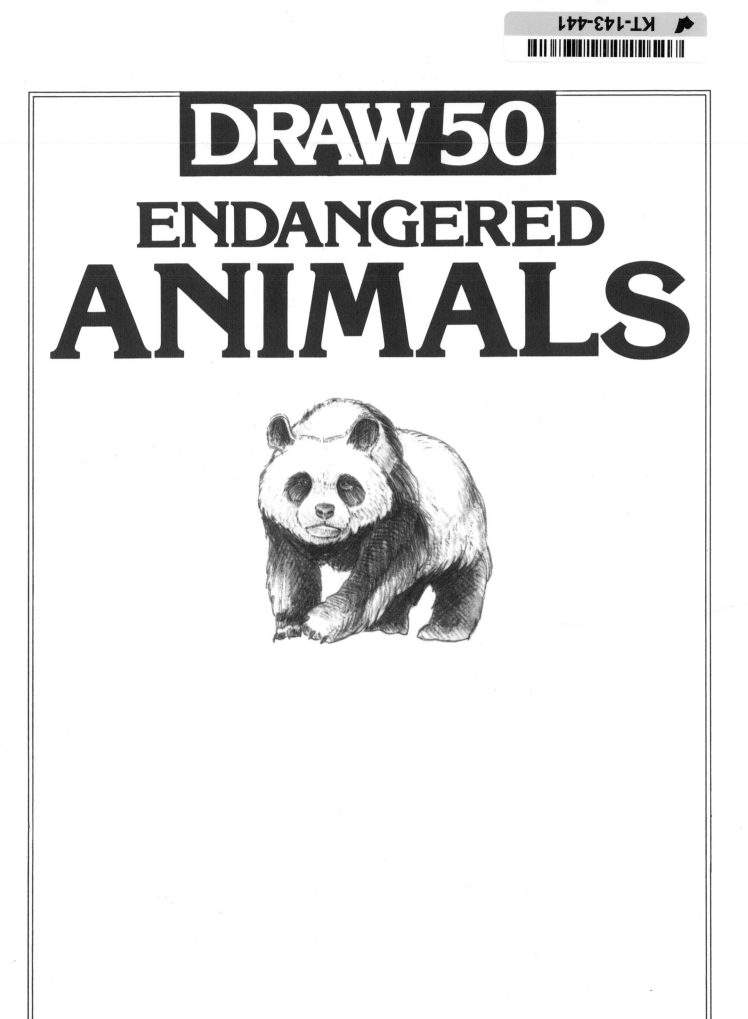

DRAW 50
ENDANGERED
ANIMALS

LEE J. AMES
AND
WARREN BUDD

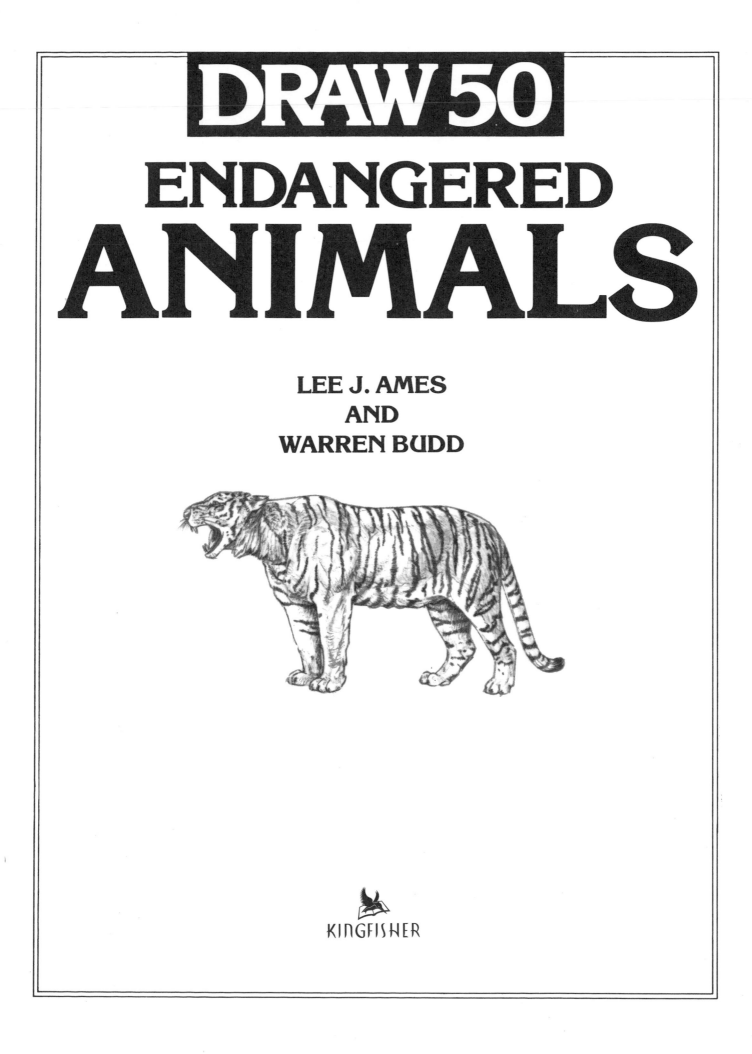

KINGFISHER

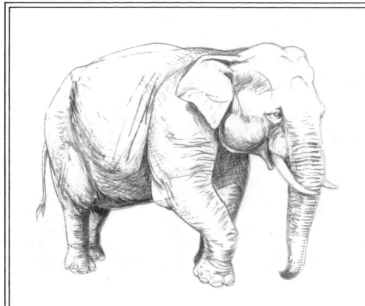

KINGFISHER
Kingfisher Publications Plc
New Penderel House, 283-288 High Holborn
London WC1V 7HZ
www.kingfisherpub.com

First published in Great Britain in 1993
by Kingfisher Publications Plc
Published by arrangement with Doubleday,
a division of Bantam Doubleday Dell Publishing Group, Inc.

10 9 8 7 6

TS2/0504/AJT/CLSN(HBM)/110WFO/F

A catalogue record for this book
is available from the British Library

ISBN 1 85697 066 3

Phototypeset by Rowland Phototypesetting Limited
Bury St Edmunds, Suffolk
Printed in India.

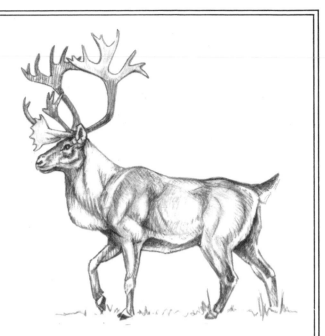

This book is dedicated, with deep
concern, to us all. For we, too,
are endangered.

TO THE READER

This book will show you a way to draw endangered animals. You need not start with the first illustration. Choose whichever you wish. When you have chosen, follow the step-by-step method shown. *Very lightly* and *carefully*, sketch out step number one. However, this step, which is the easiest, should be done most carefully. Step number two is added on top of step number one, also lightly and also very carefully. Step number three is sketched right on top of numbers one and two. Continue in this way to the last step.

It may seem strange to ask you to be extra careful when you are drawing what seem to be the easiest first steps, but this is most important because a careless mistake at the beginning may spoil the whole picture at the end. As you sketch out a step, watch the spaces between the lines, as well as the lines themselves, and see that they are the same. After each step, you may want to lighten your work by pressing it with a plastic, or 'putty' rubber (available at art supply shops).

When you have finished, you may want to redo the final step in India ink with a fine brush or pen–or use a fine pointed felt-tip pen. When the ink is dry, use the plastic rubber to clean off the pencil lines. The rubber will not affect the ink.

Continued over page

Here are some suggestions: In the first few steps, even when all seems quite correct, you might do well to hold your work up to a mirror. Sometimes the mirror shows that you've twisted the drawing off to one side without being aware of it. At first you may find it difficult to draw the egg shapes or circles, or just to make the pencil go where you want it to. Don't be discouraged. The more you practise, the more you will develop control. Use a compass to help you if you wish; professional artists do!

The only equipment you will need will be a medium or soft pencil, paper, the plastic rubber and, if you wish, a compass, pen or brush and India ink–or a felt-tip pen. The first steps in this book are shown darker than necessary so that they can be clearly seen. (Keep your work very light.)

Remember, this book presents only one method of drawing. In a most enjoyable way, it will help you to develop a certain skill and control. But there are many other ways of drawing to which you can apply this skill, and the more of them you try, the more interesting your drawings will be.

Lee J. Ames

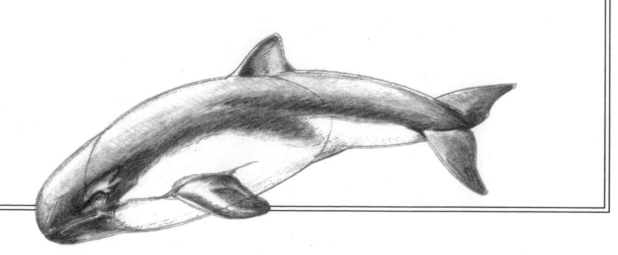

TO THE PARENT OR TEACHER

Drawing, like any other skill, requires practice and discipline. But this does not mean that rewards cannot be found along every step of the way.

While contemporary methods of art instruction rightly emphasize freedom of expression and experimentation, they often lose sight of a very basic, traditional and valuable approach: the 'follow me, step-by-step' way that I learned as a youth.

Just as a beginning musician is given simple, beautiful melodies to play, so too the young artist needs to gain a sense of satisfaction and pride in his or her work as soon as possible. The 'do as I do' steps that I have laid out here provide the opportunity to mimic finished images, images the young artist is eager to draw.

Mimicry is prerequisite for developing creativity. We learn the use of our tools through mimicry, and once we have those tools we are free to express ourselves in whatever fashion we choose. The use of this book will help lay a solid foundation for a child, one that can be continued with other books in the *Draw 50* series, or even used to complement different approaches to drawing.

Above all, the joy of making a credible, attractive image will encourage the child to continue and grow as an artist, giving him even more of a sense of pride and accomplishment when his friends say, 'Peter can draw an elephant better than anyone else!'

Lee J. Ames

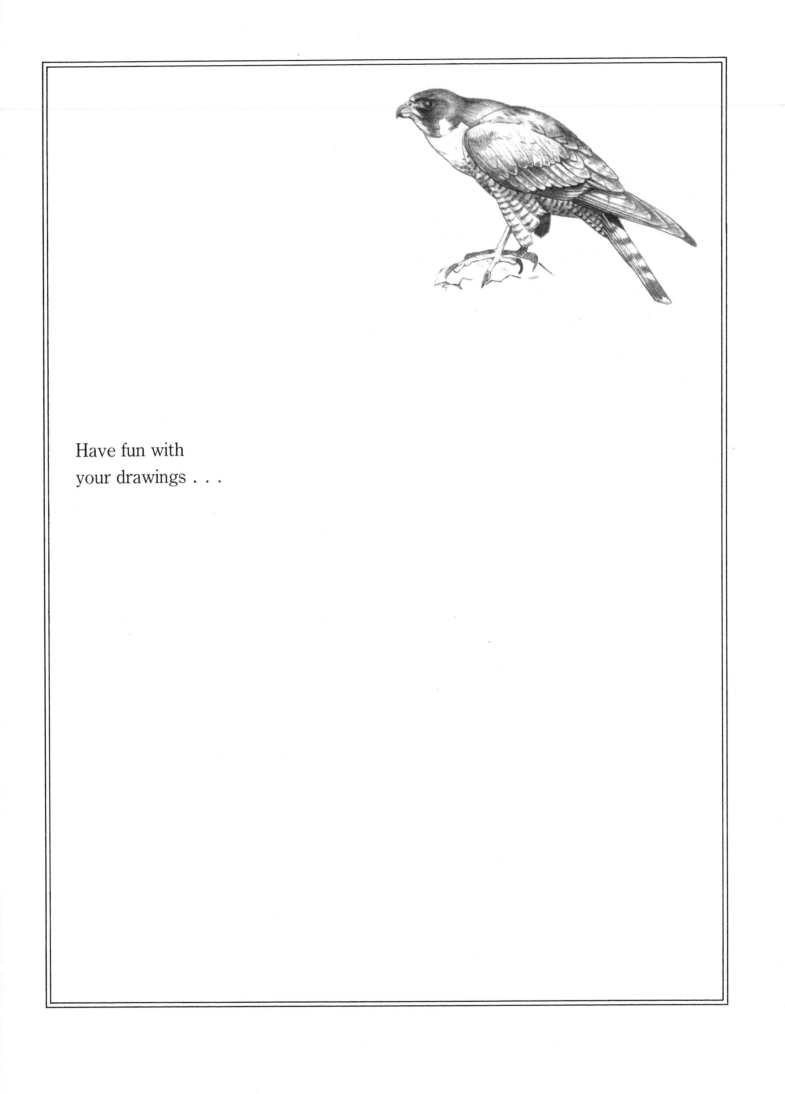

Have fun with
your drawings . . .

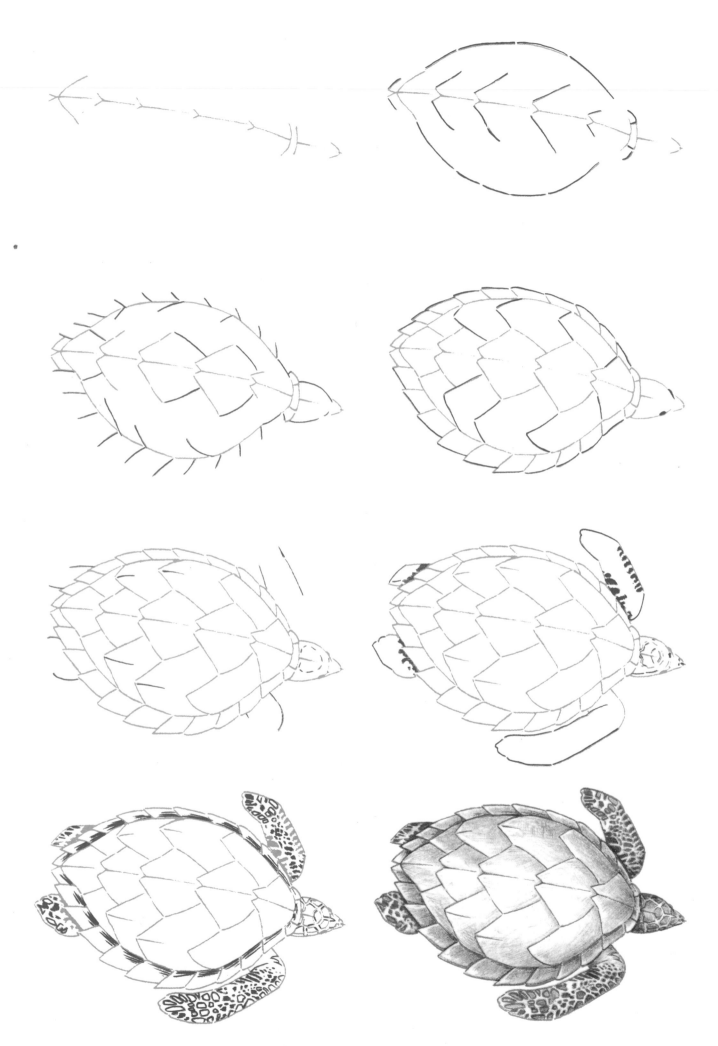

Hawksbill Turtle

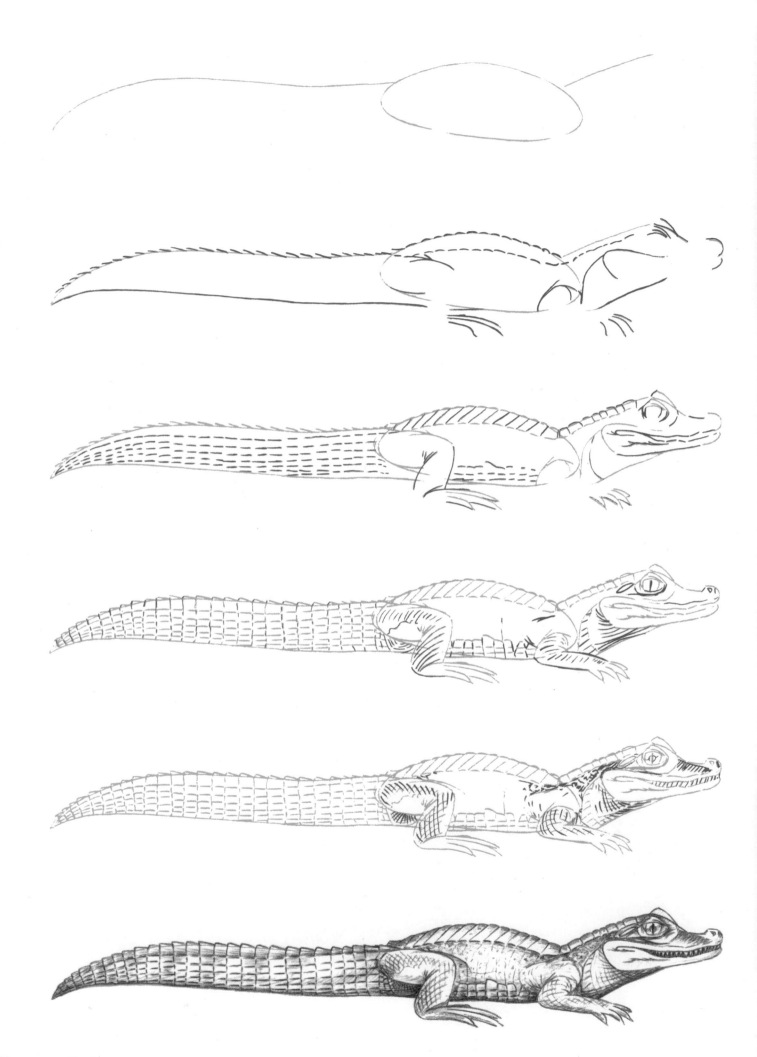

Yacare Caiman

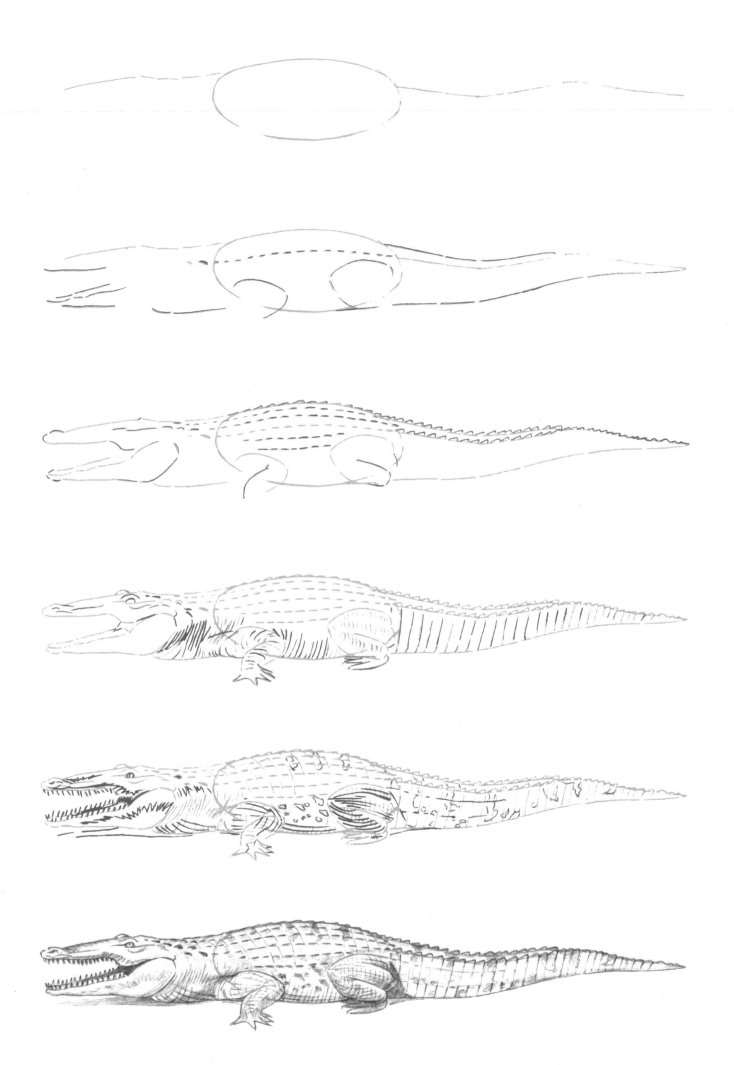

American Crocodile

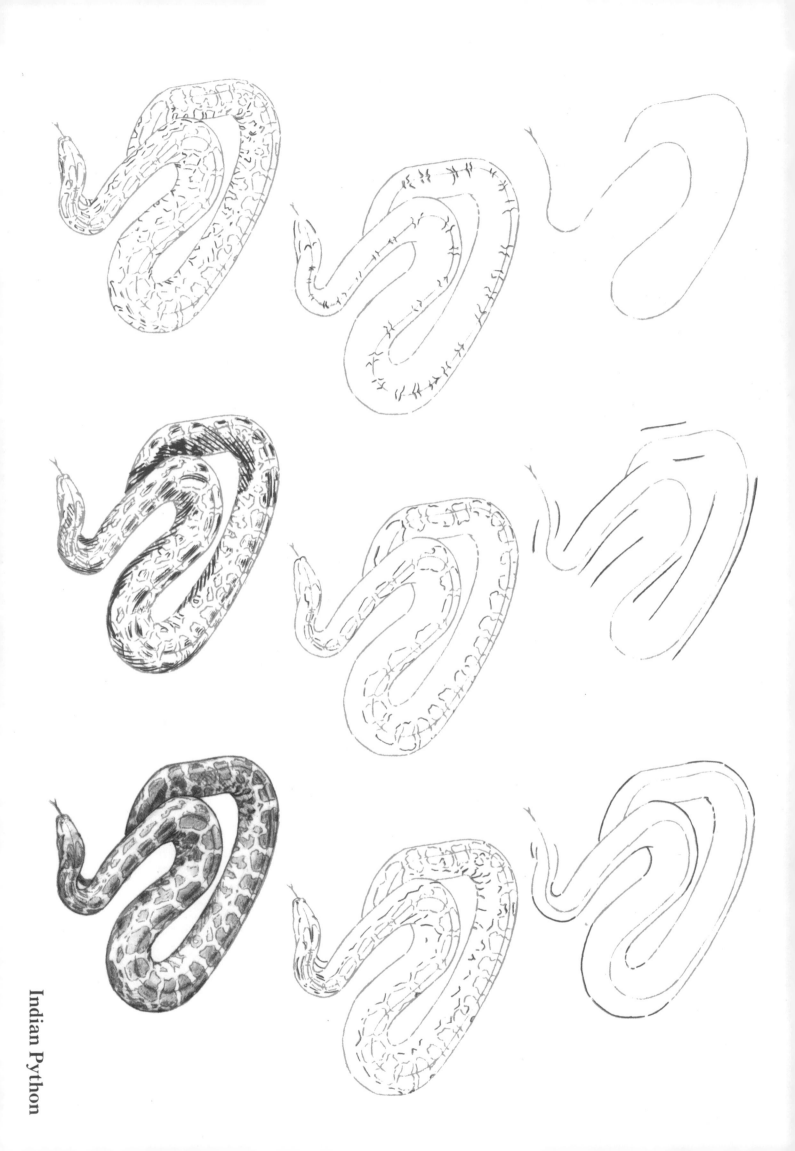

Indian Python

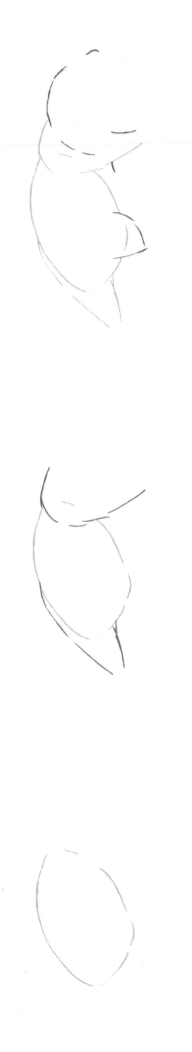

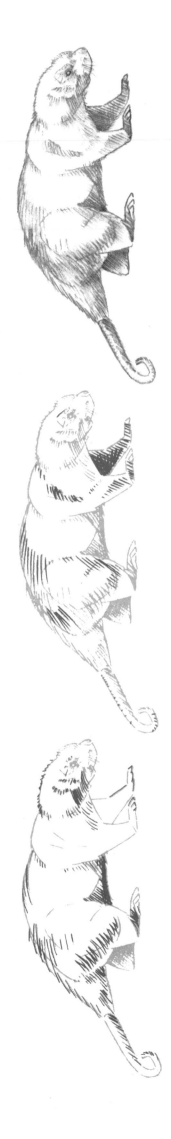

Thin-Spined Porcupine

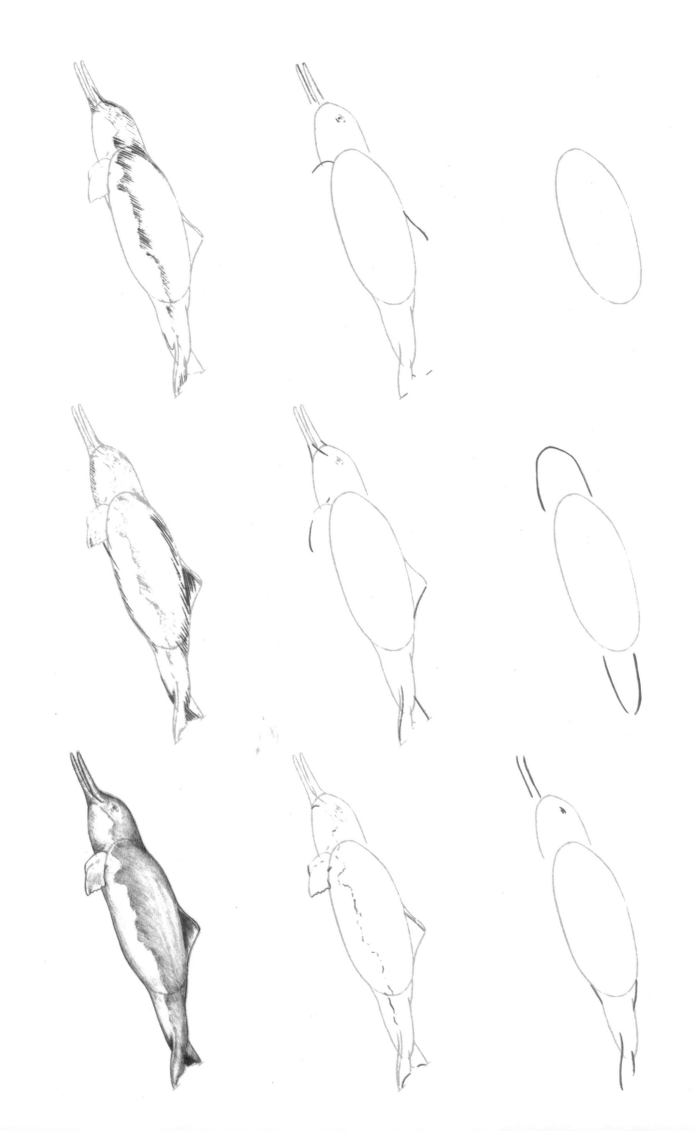

Chinese River Dolphin

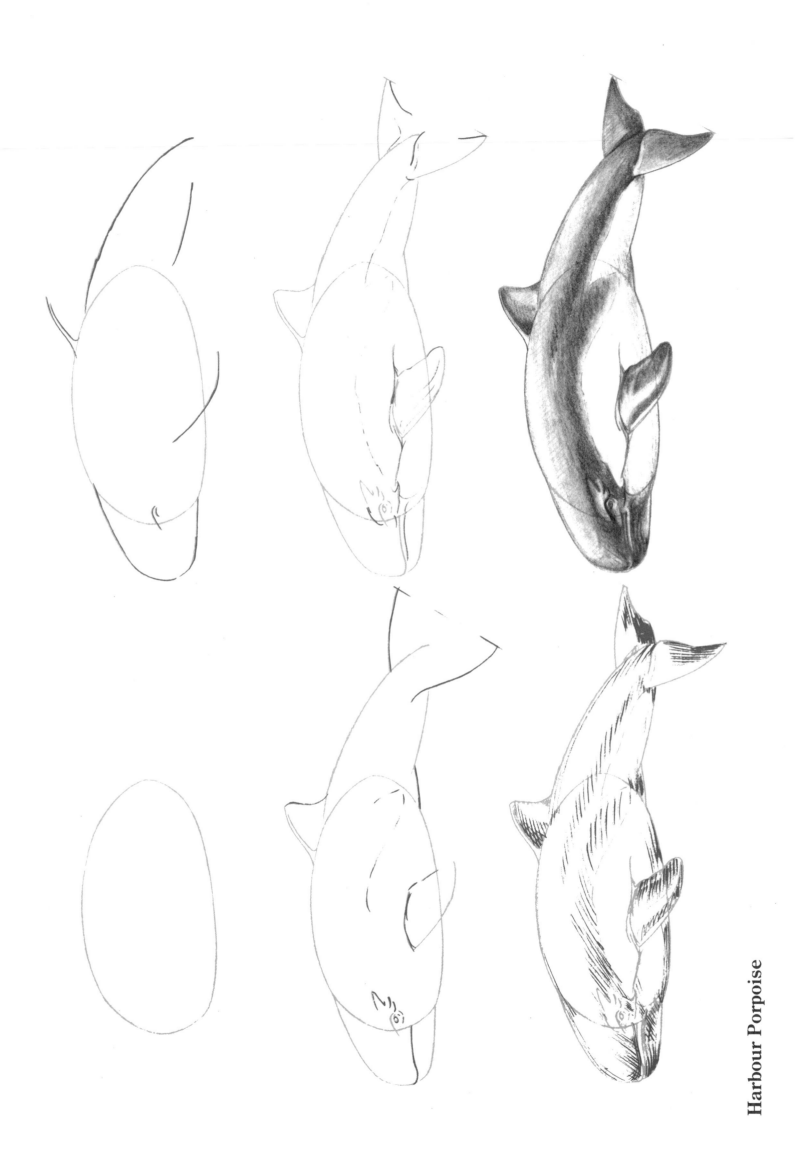

Harbour Porpoise

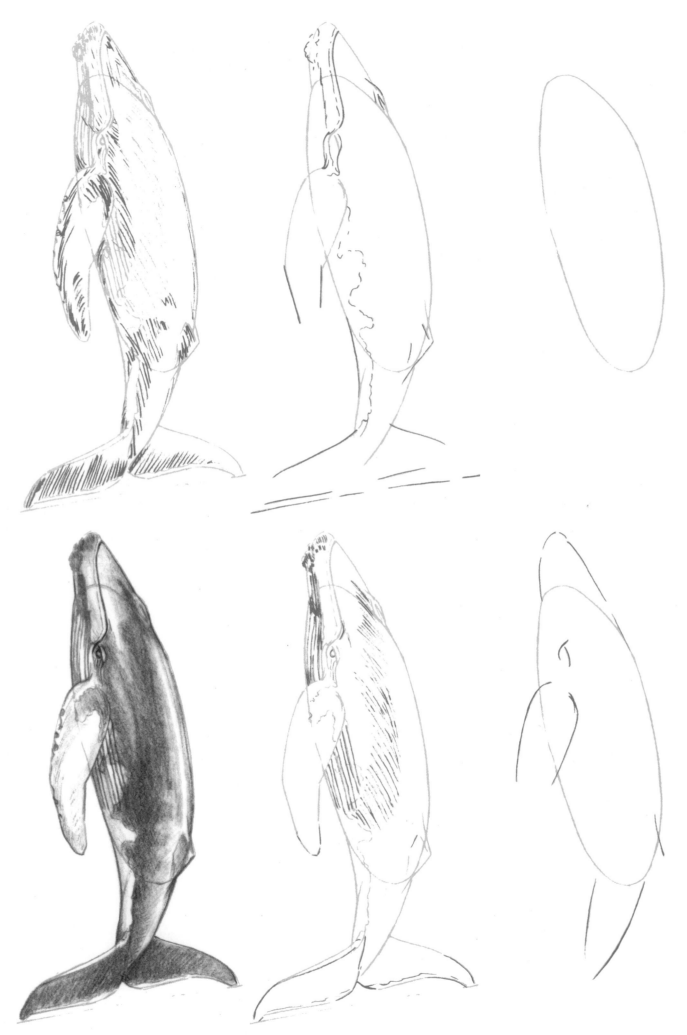

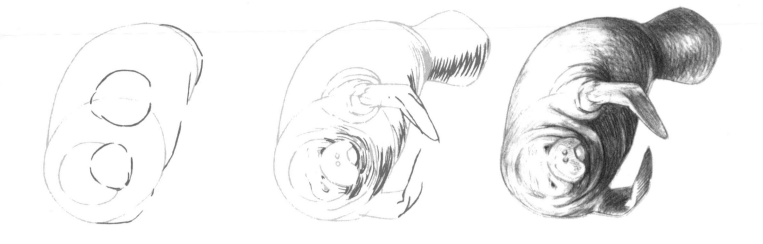

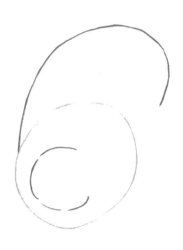

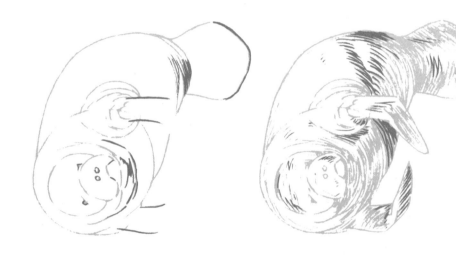

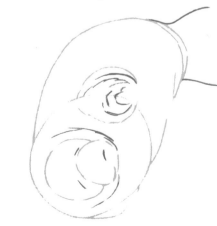

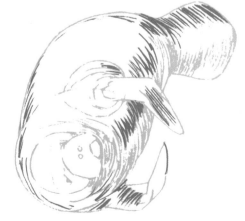

West Indian Manatee

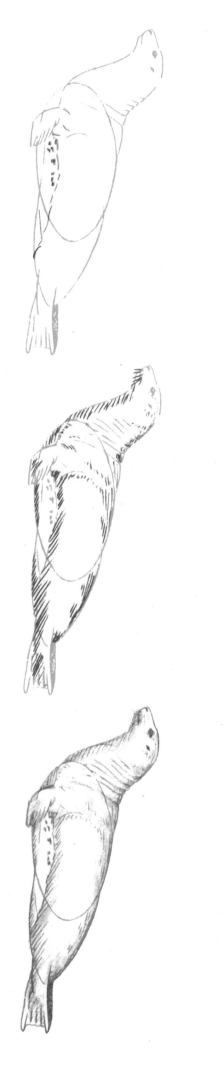
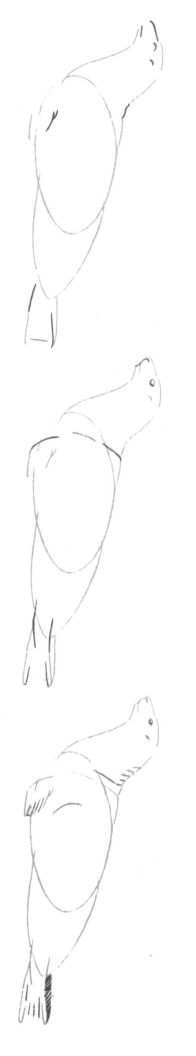

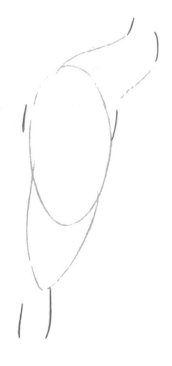

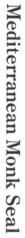Mediterranean Monk Seal

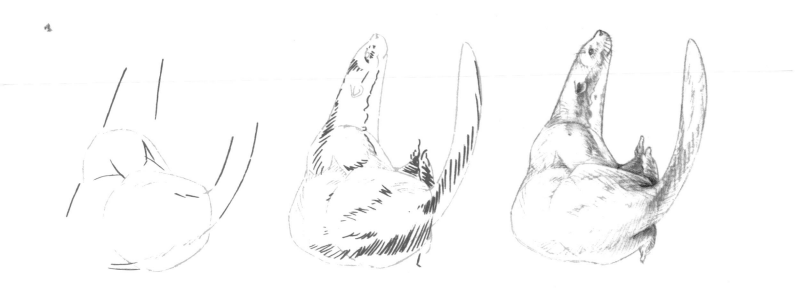

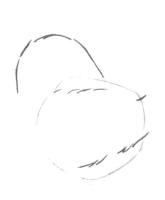
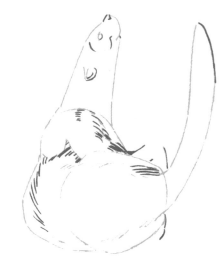
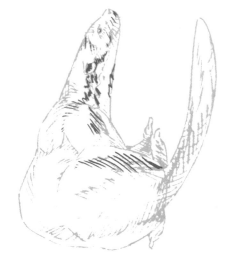

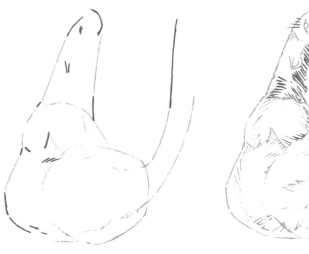
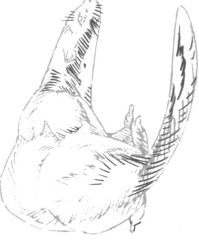

Giant Otter

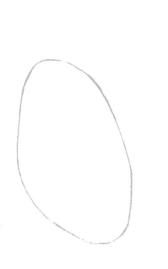
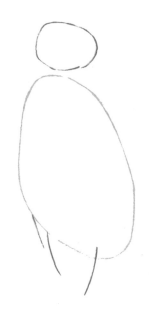
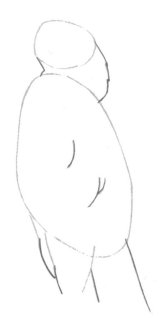
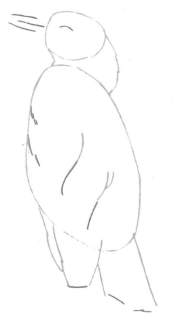
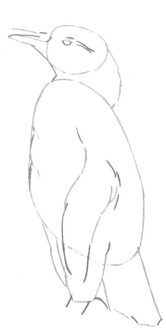
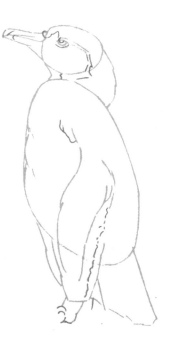
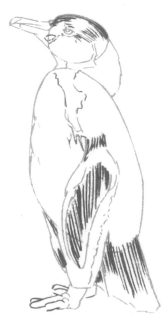
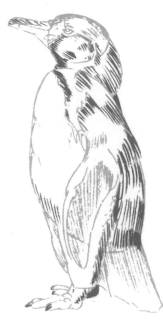
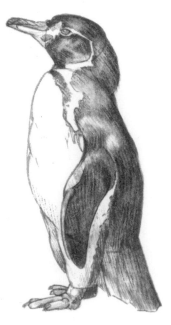

Galapagos Penguin

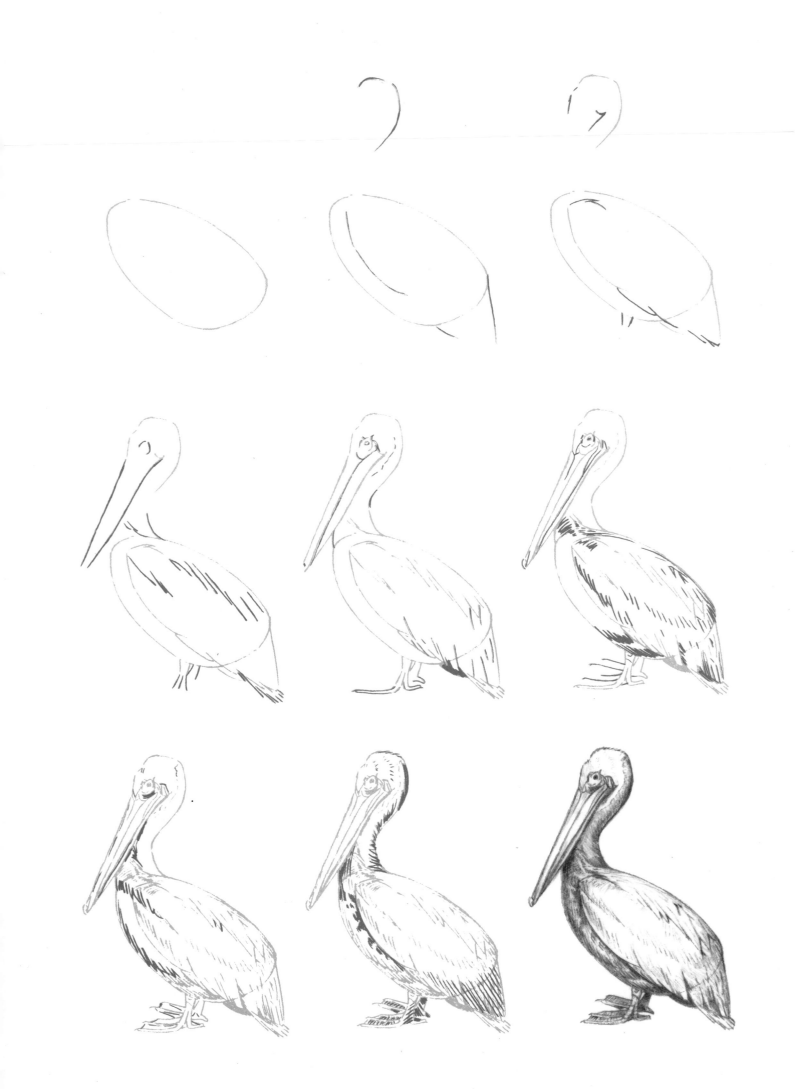

Brown Pelican

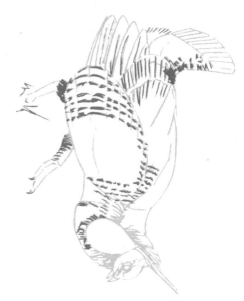
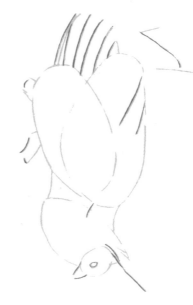

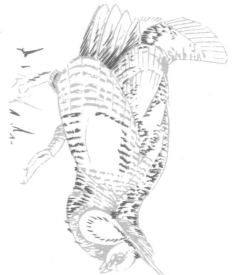
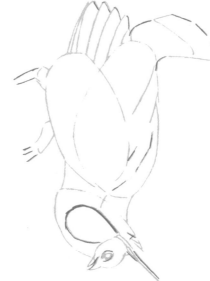
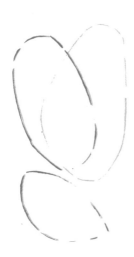

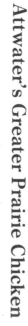

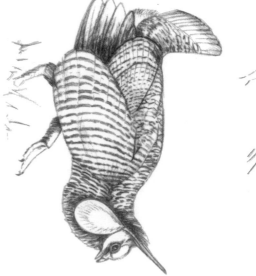
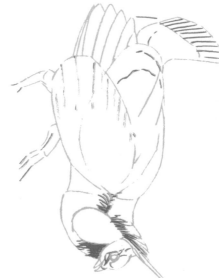
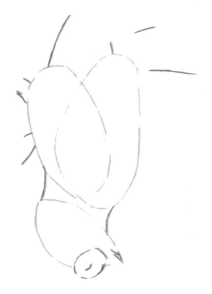

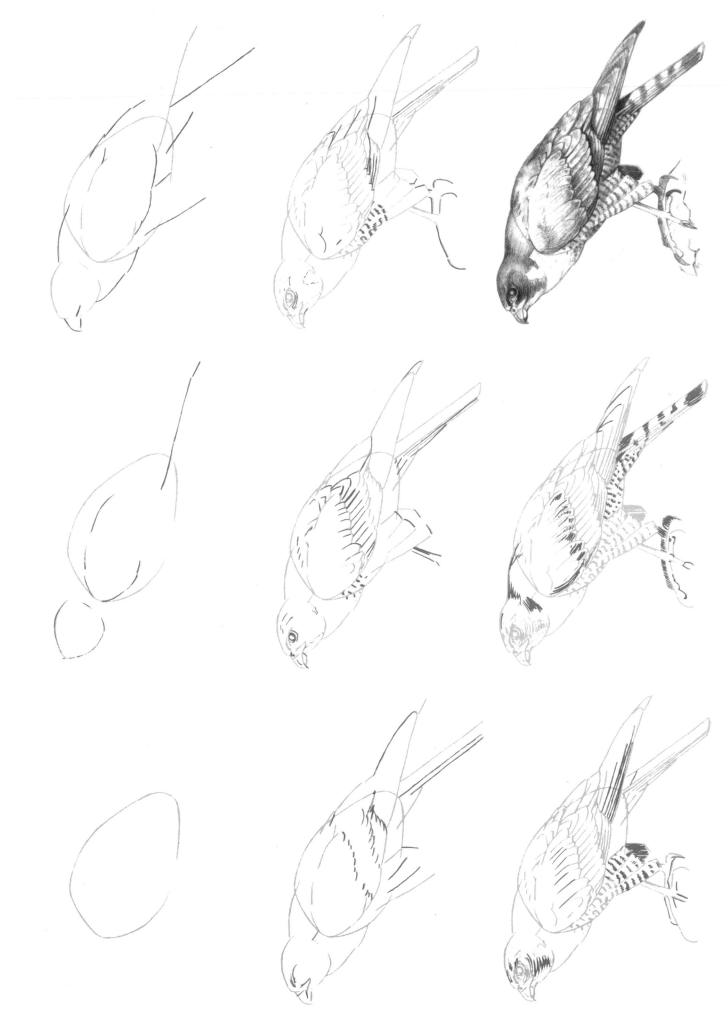

Peregrine Falcon

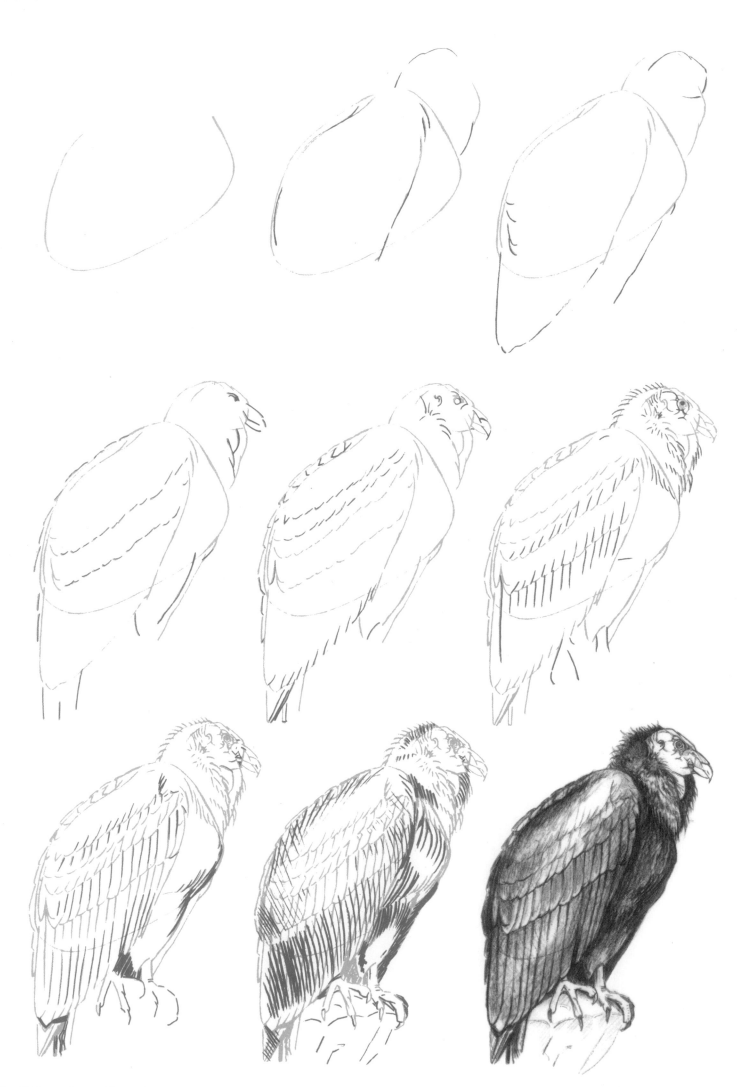

Californian Condor

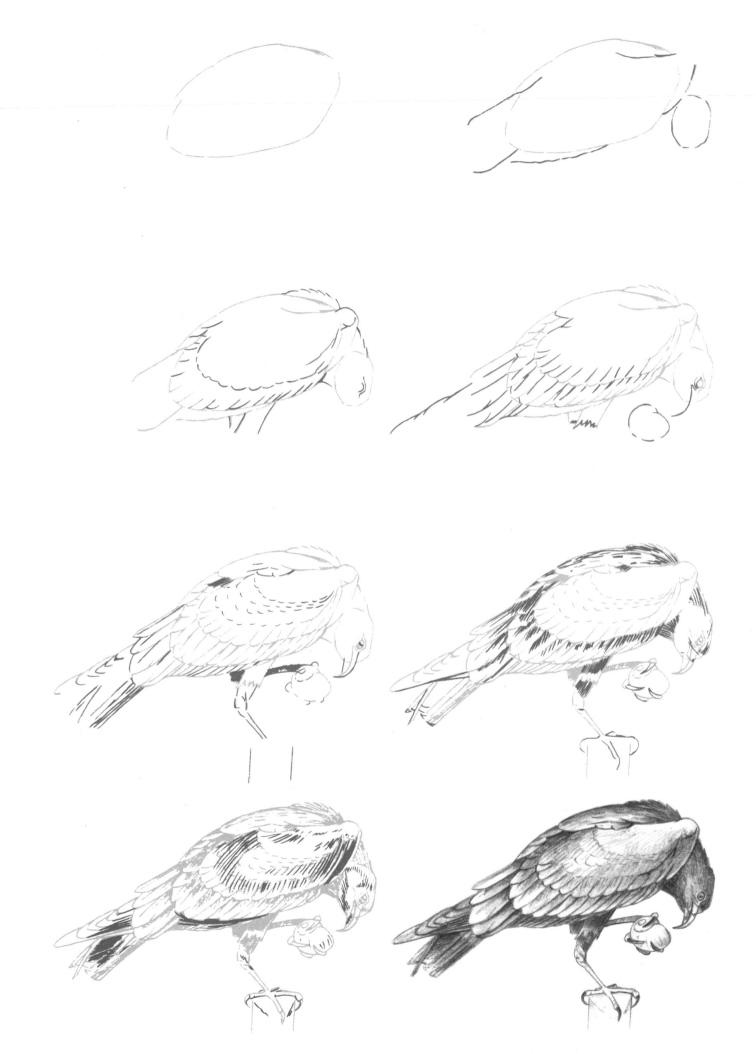

Everglades Snail Kite

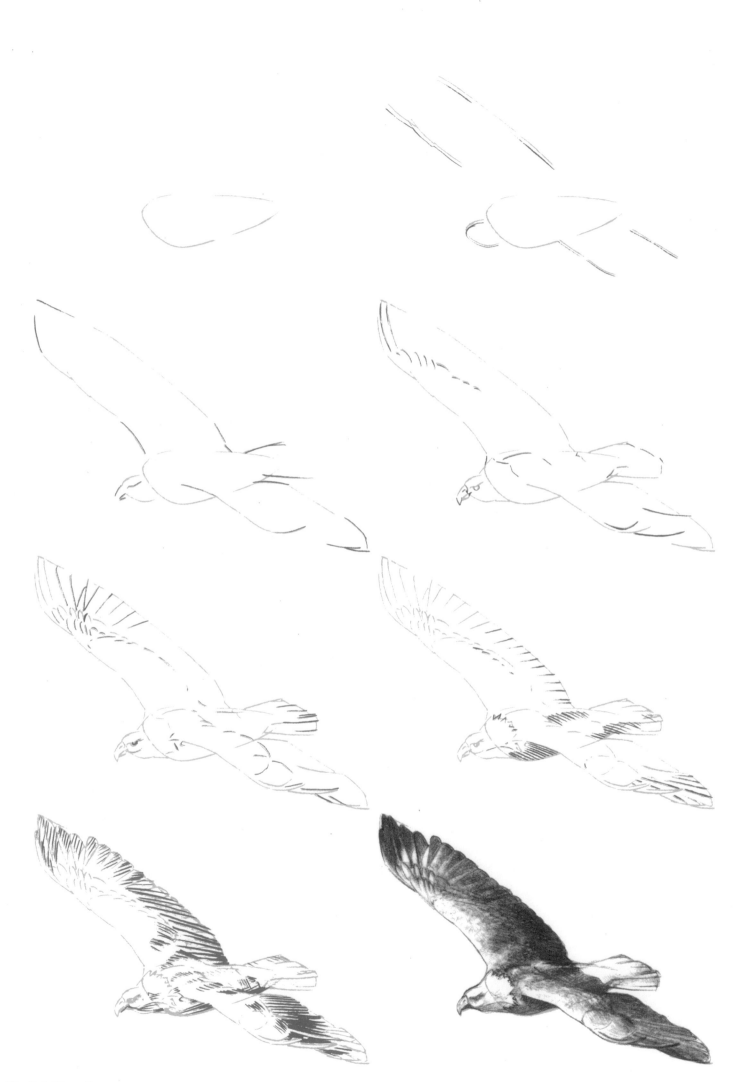

Bald Eagle

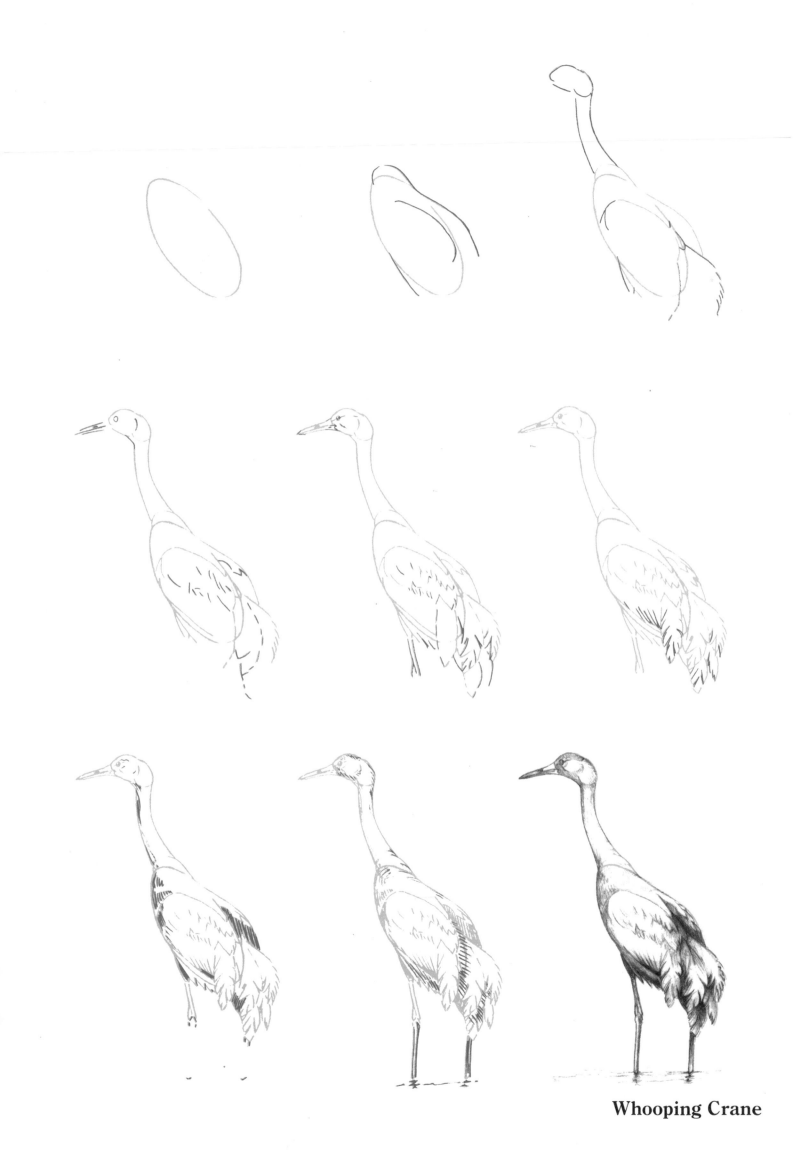

Whooping Crane

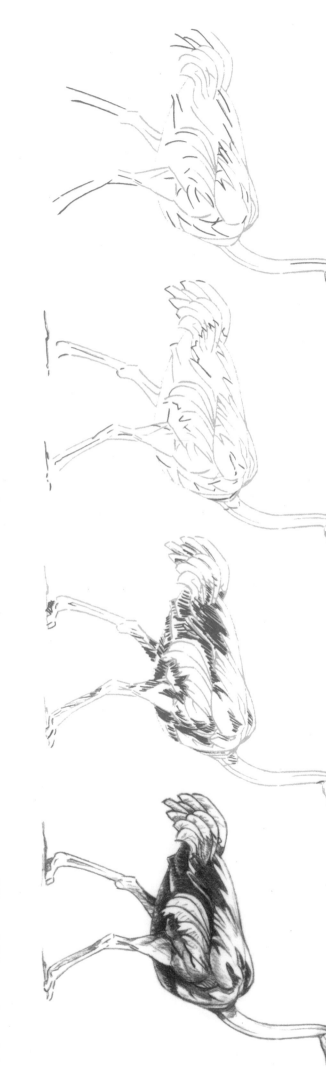

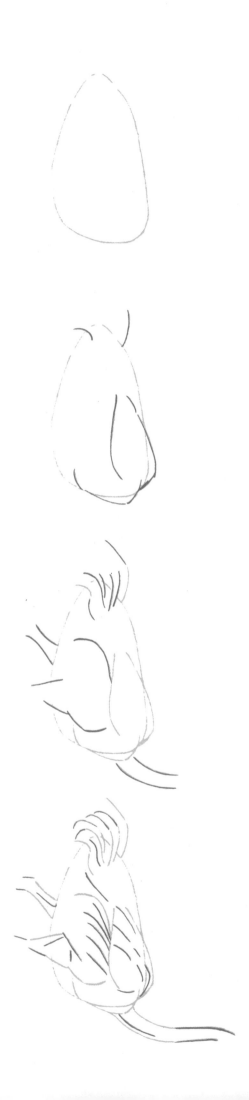

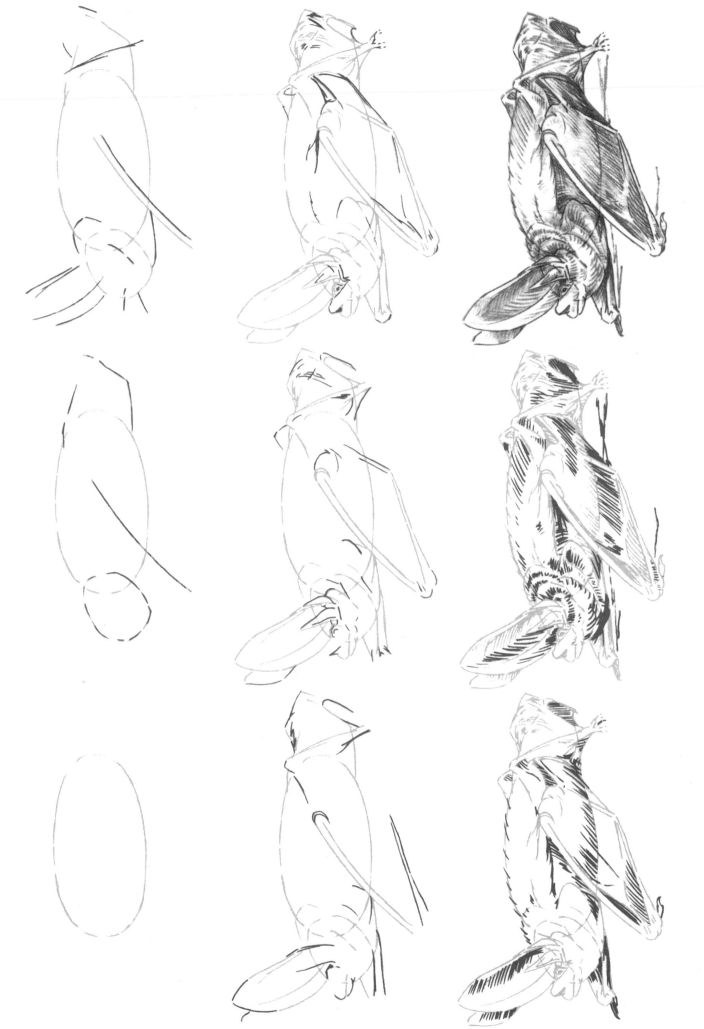

Virginia Big-Eared Bat

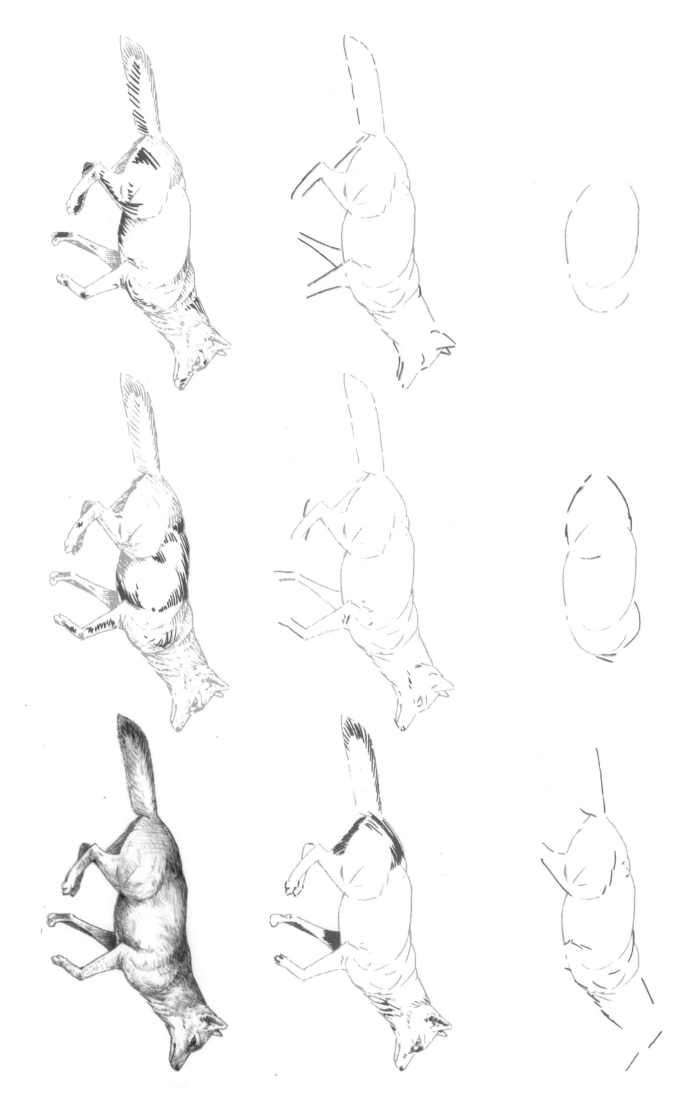

Red Wolf

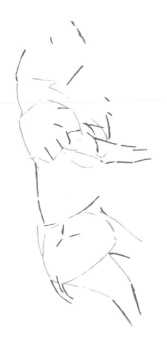
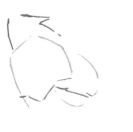
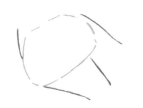

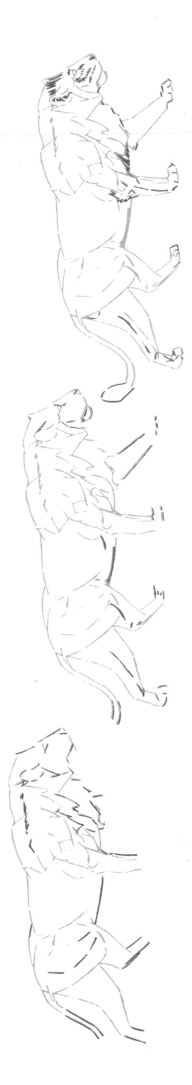
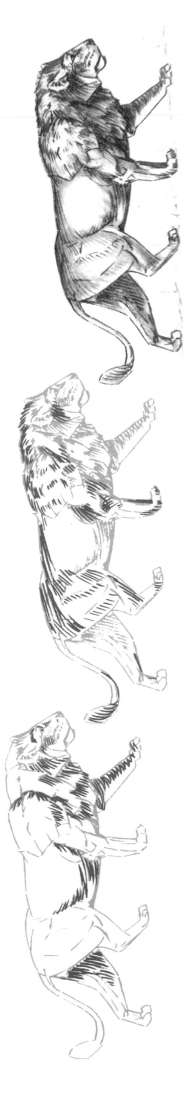

Asiatic Lion

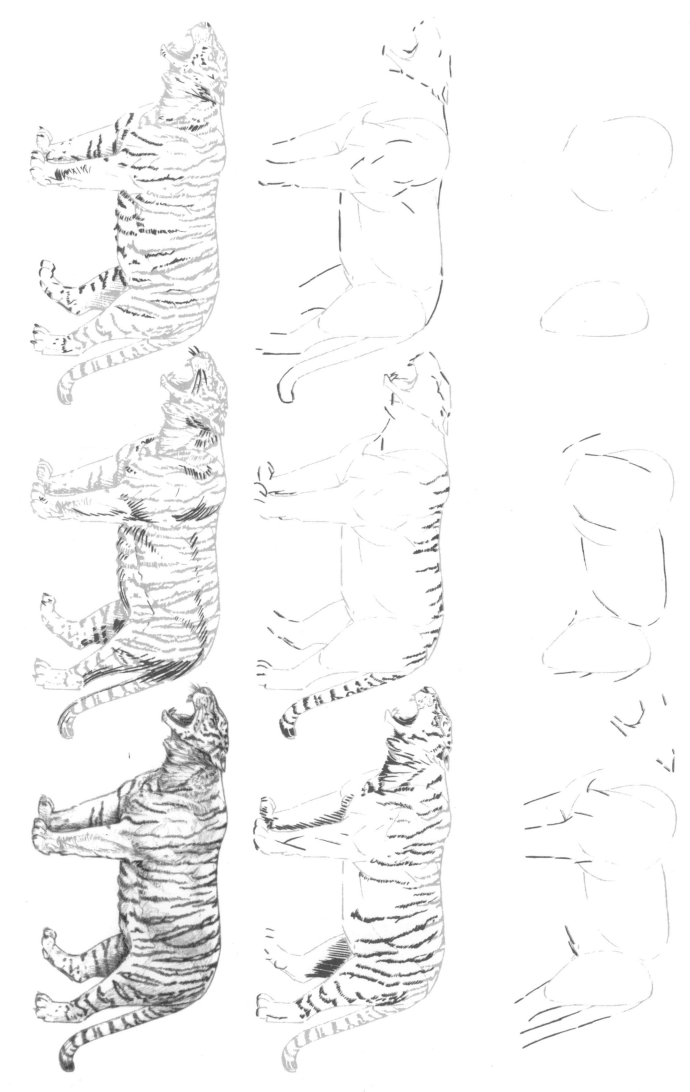

Siberian Tiger

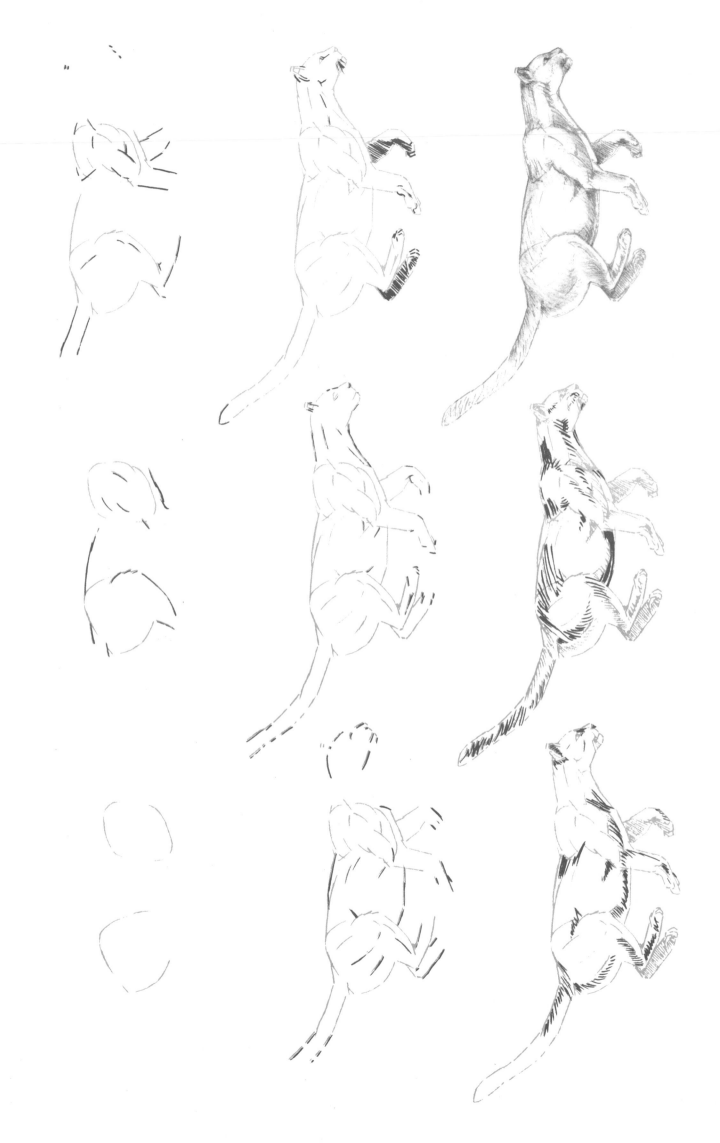

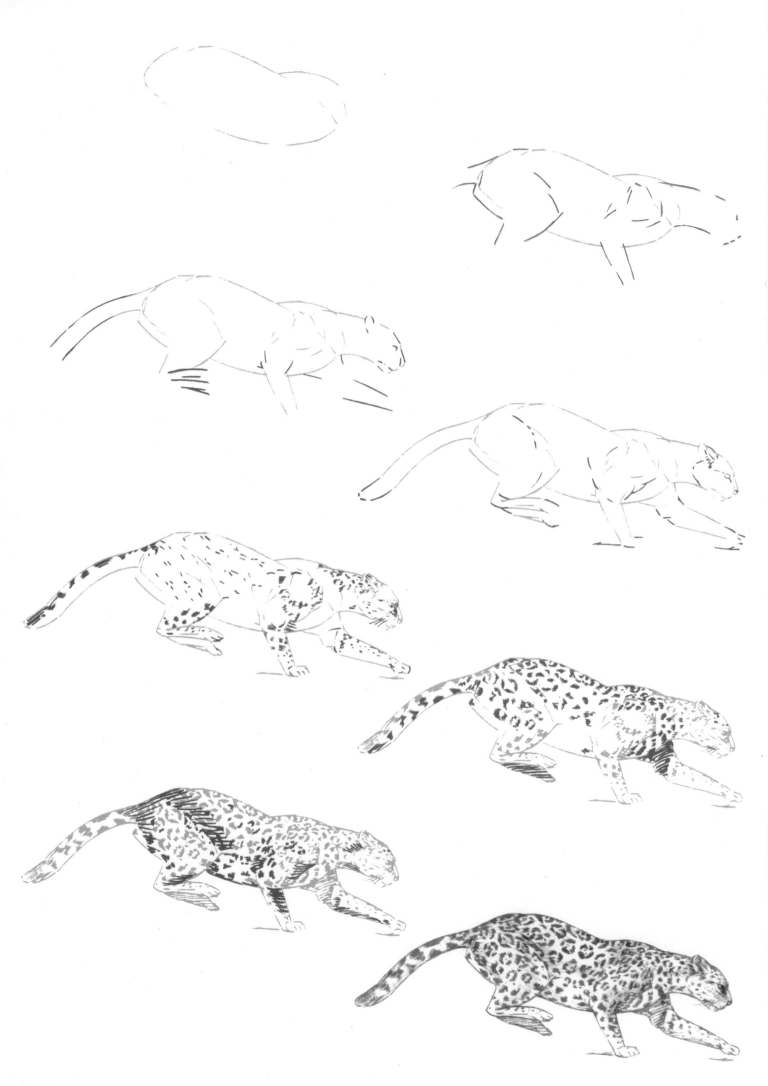

Jaguar

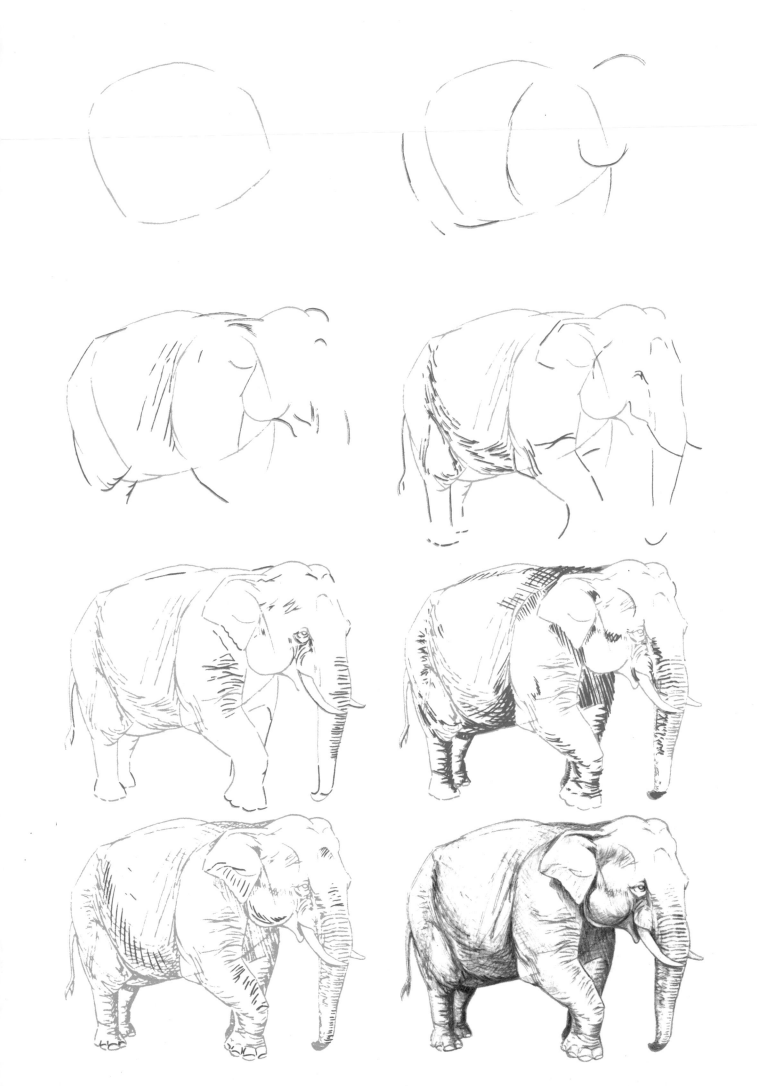

Asiatic Elephant

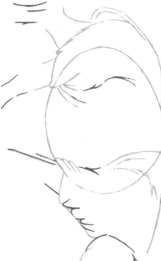

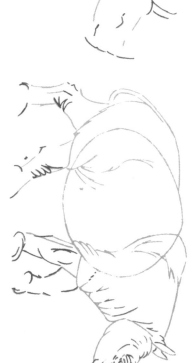

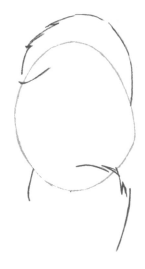

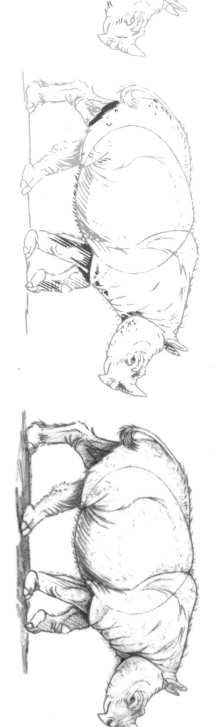

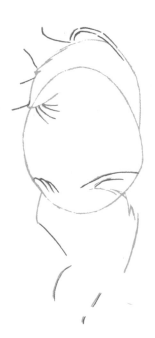

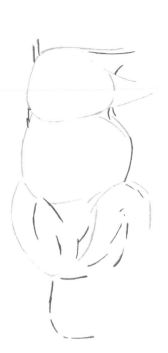
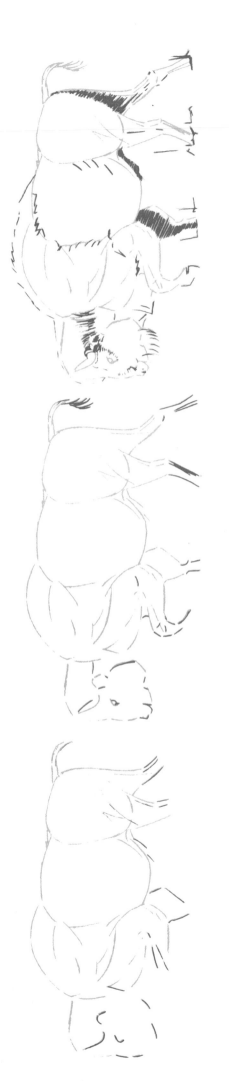
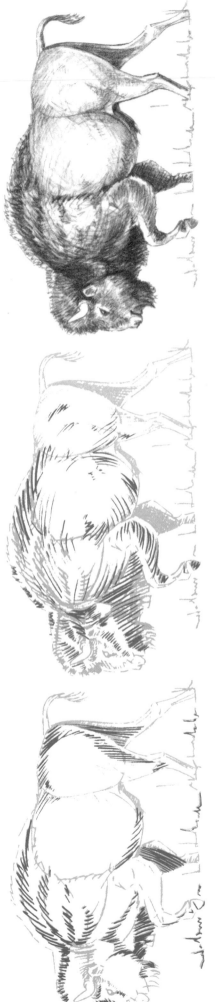
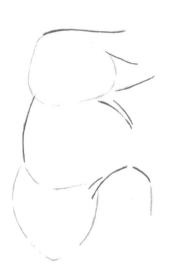

Wood Bison

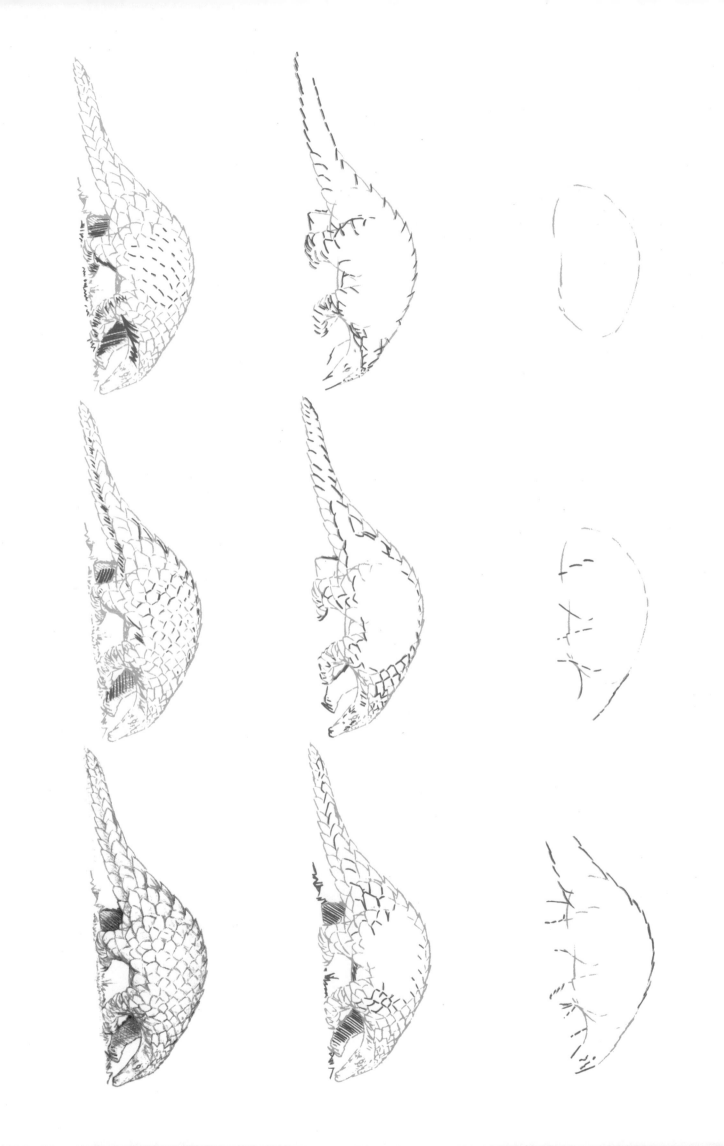

Pangolin

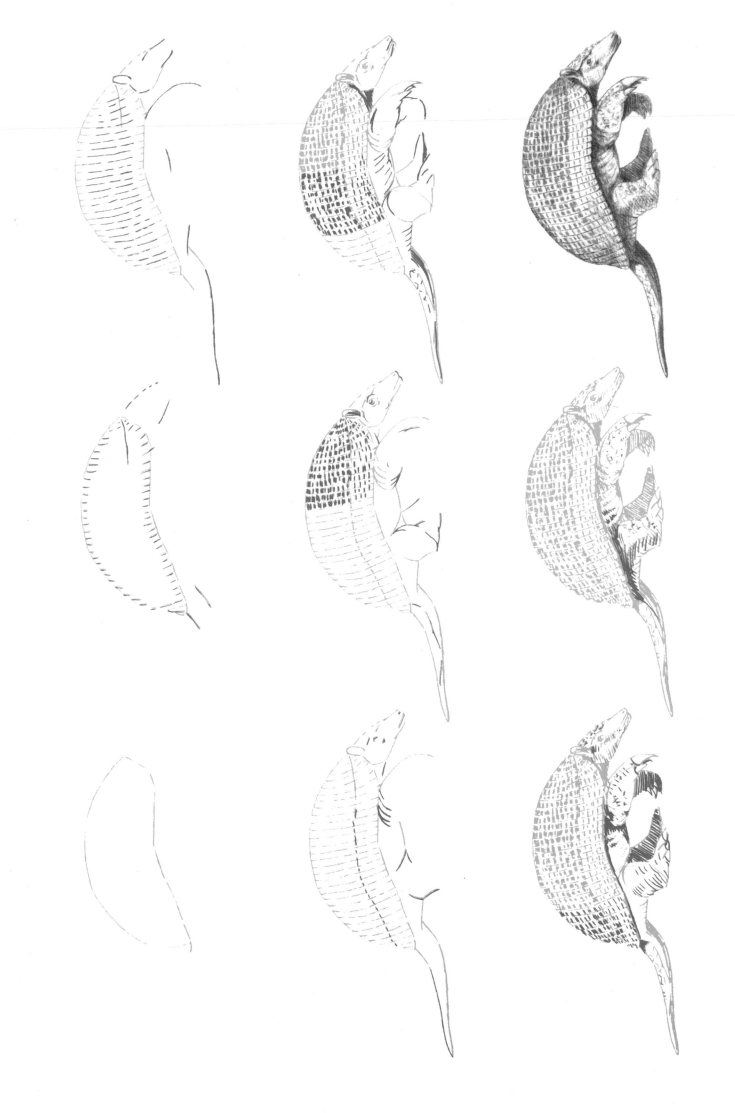

Giant Armadillo

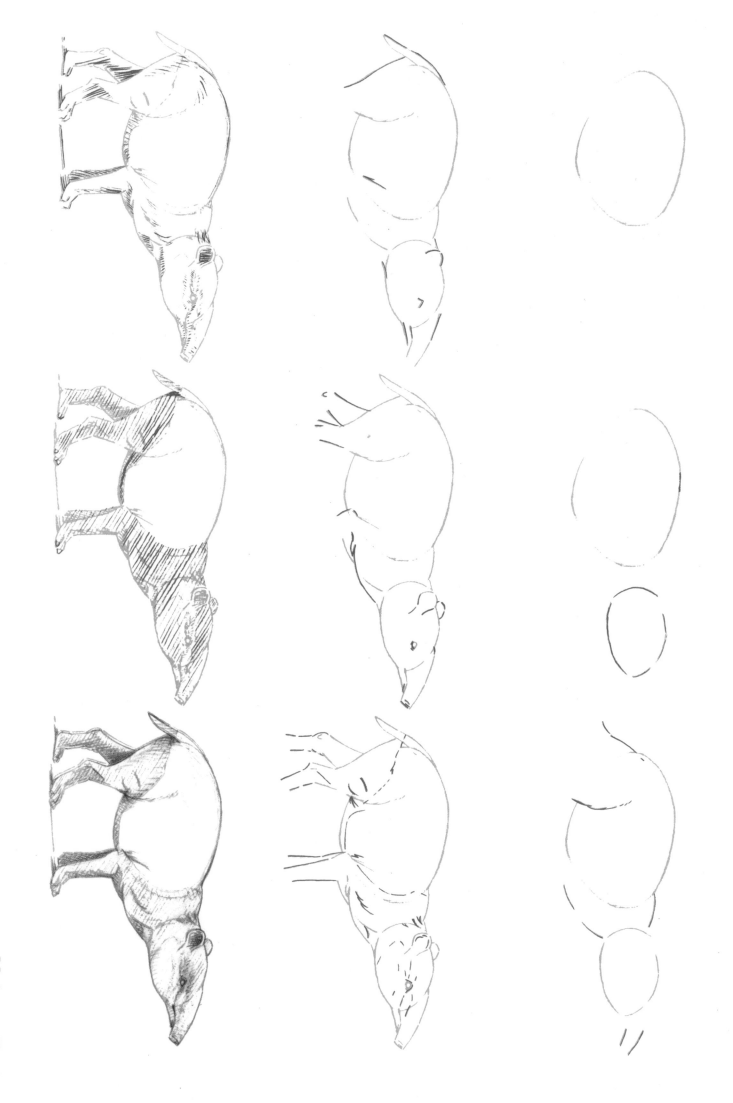

Malayan Tapir

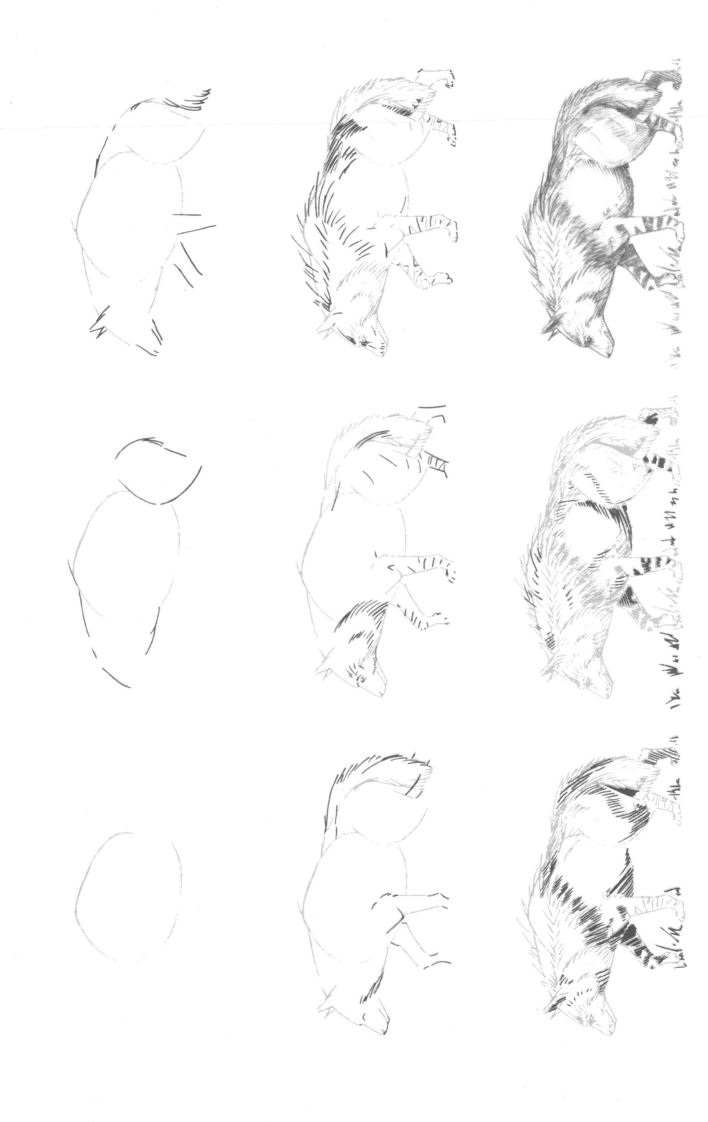

Brown Hyena

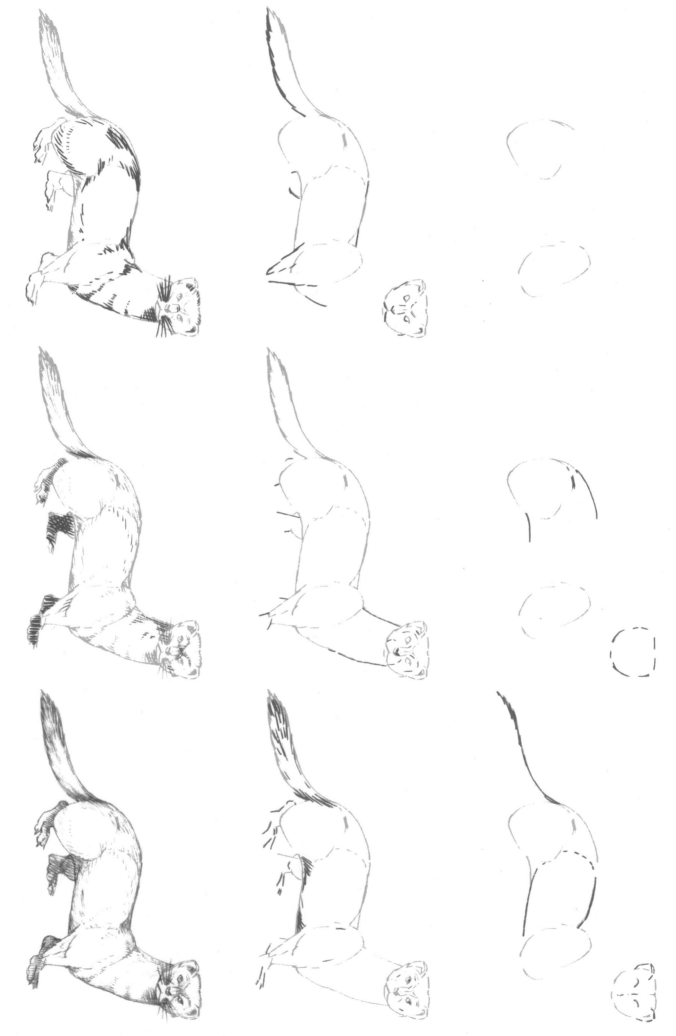

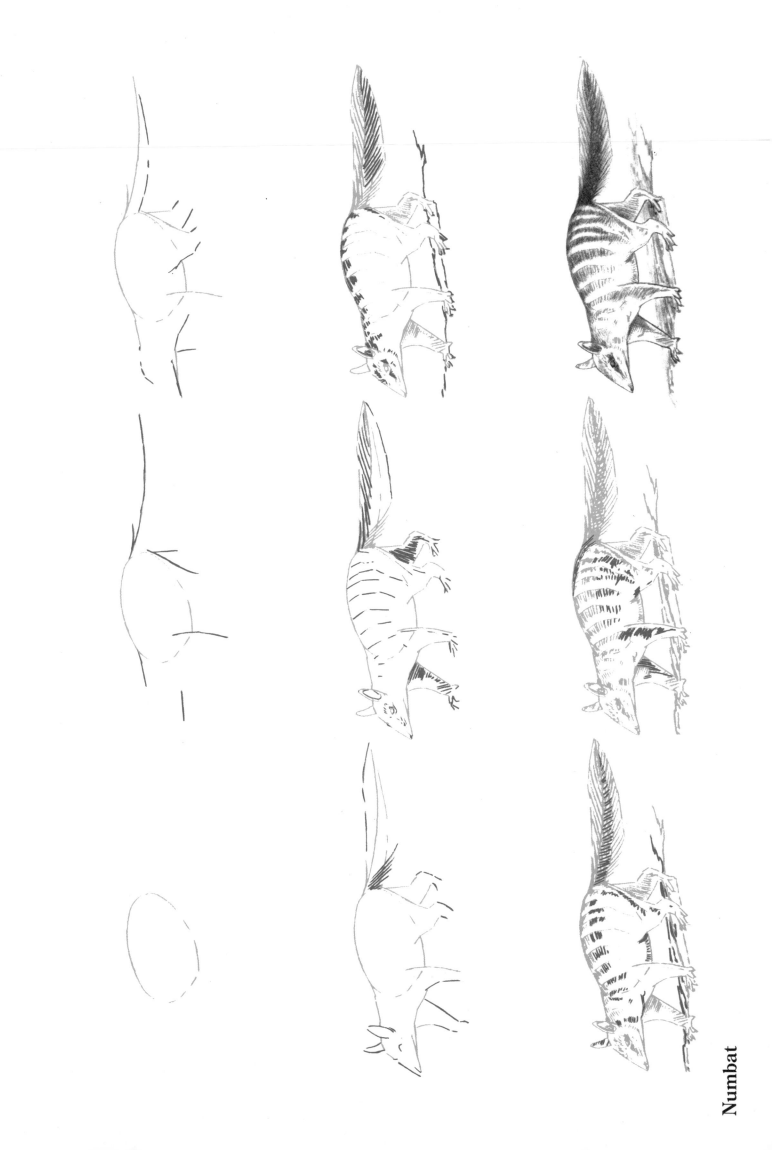

Numbat

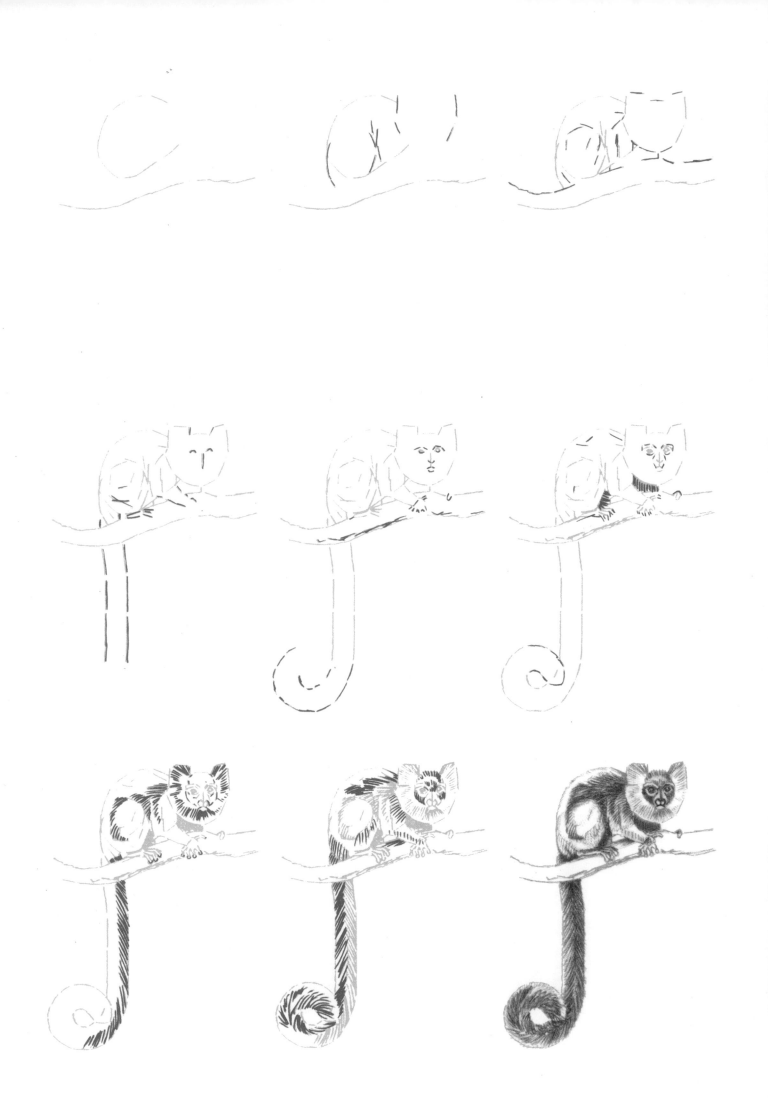

Ruffed Lemur

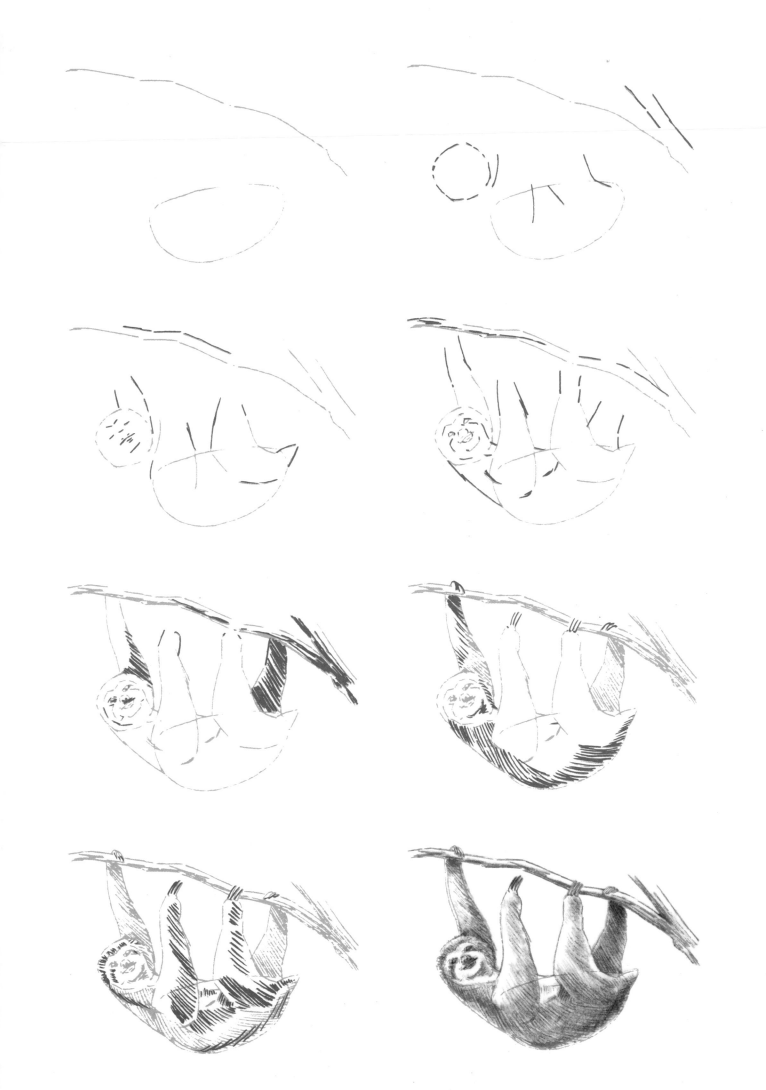

Brazilian Three-Toed Sloth

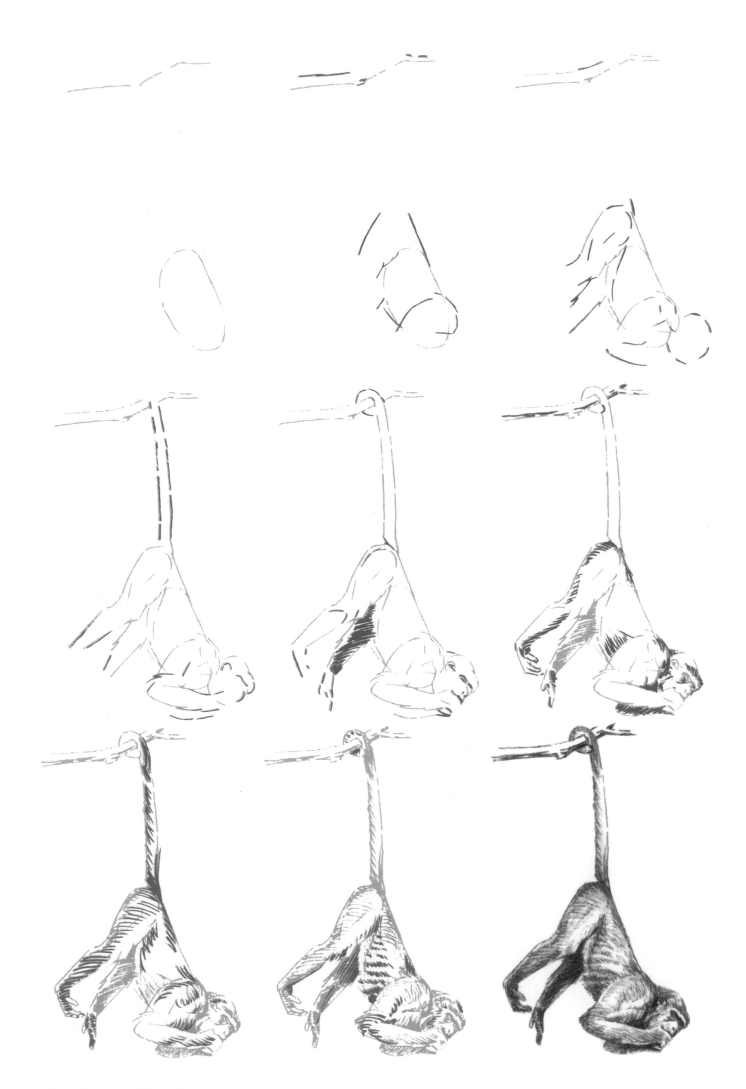

Woolly Spider Monkey

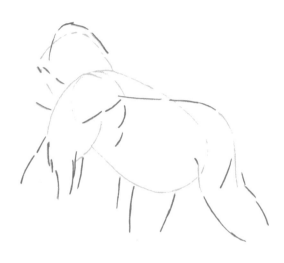 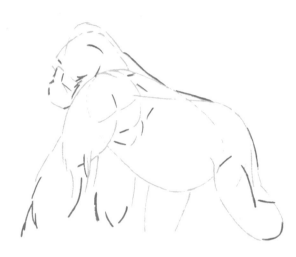

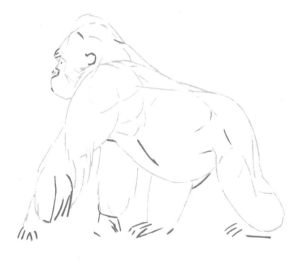 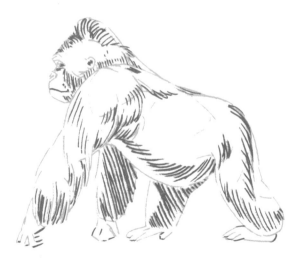

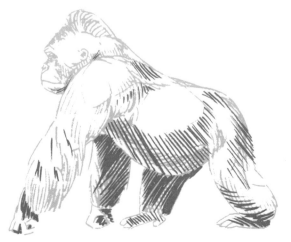 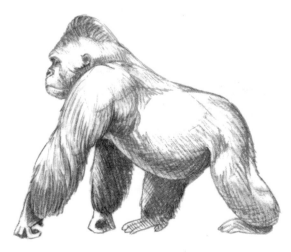

Gorilla

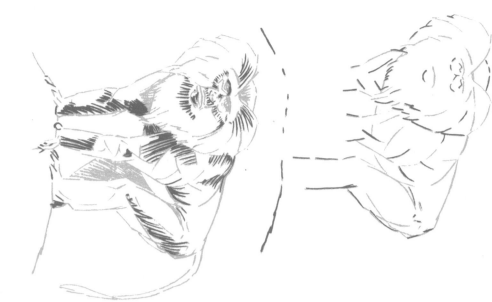

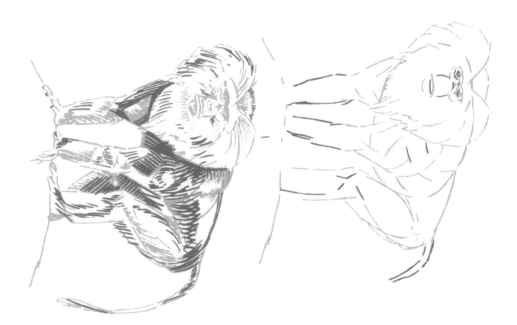

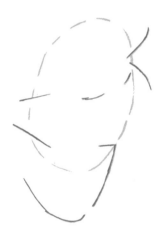

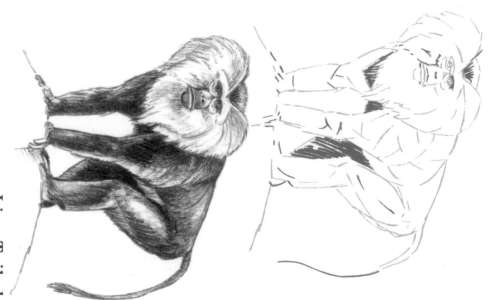

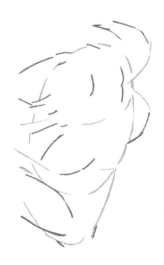

Lion-Tailed Macaque

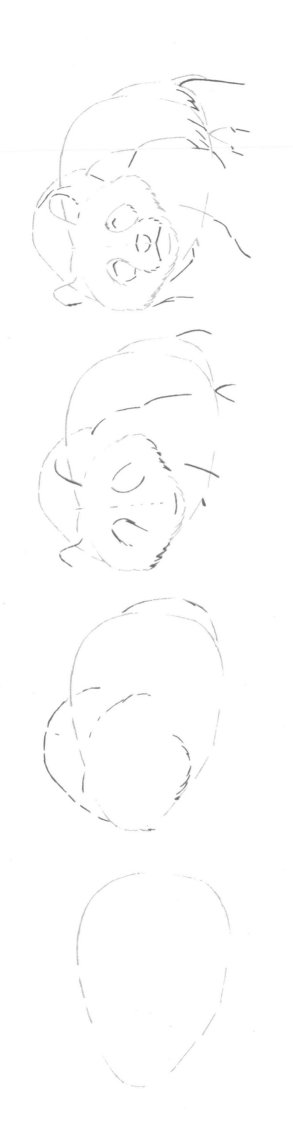
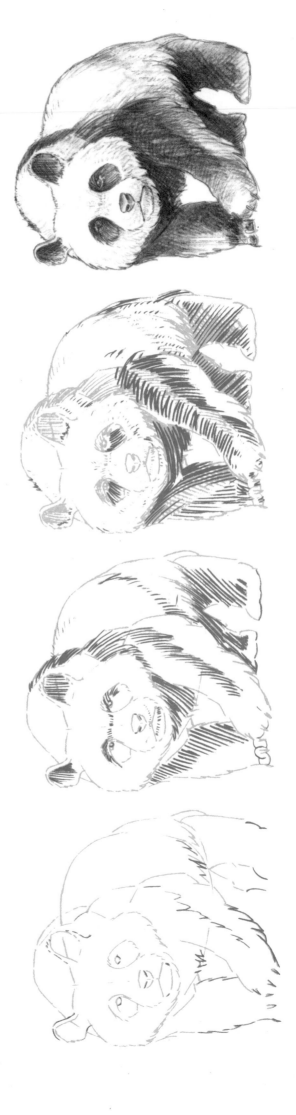

Giant Panda

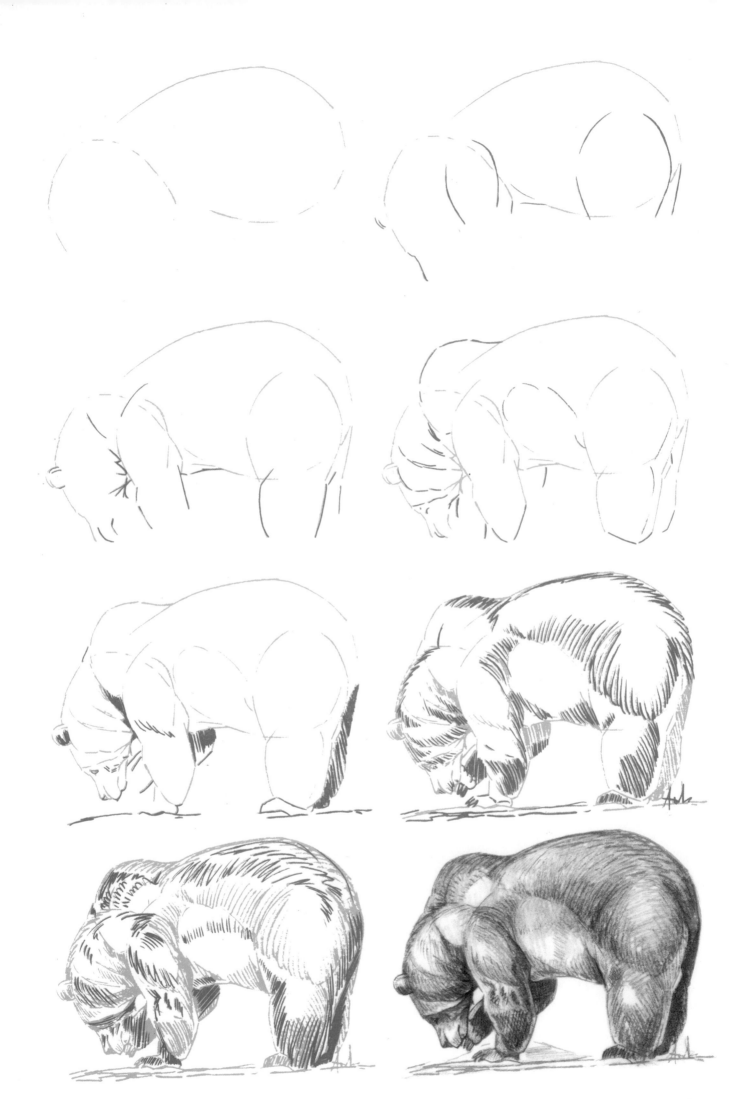

Brown Bear

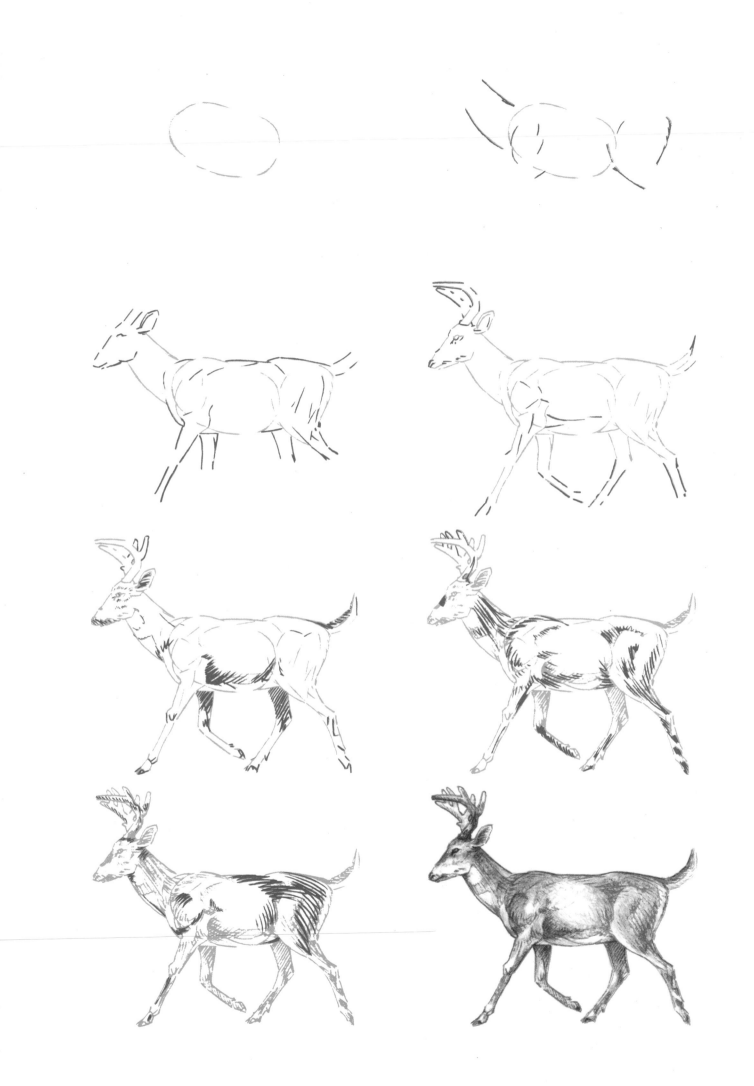

Columbian White-Tailed Deer

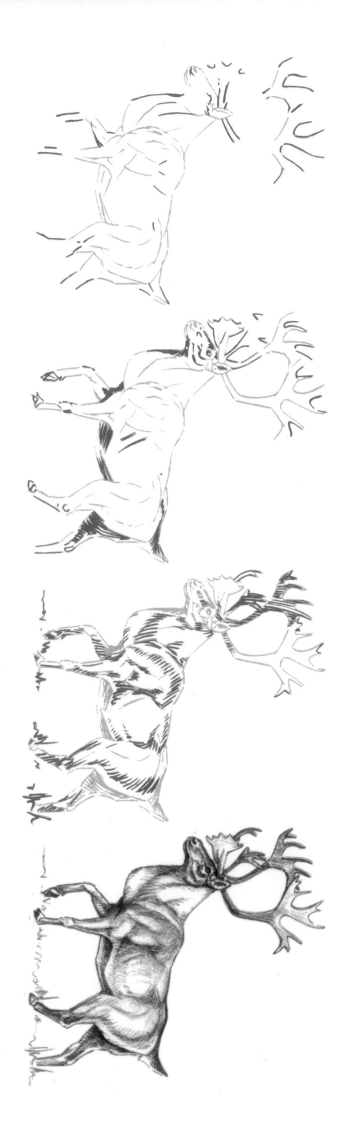

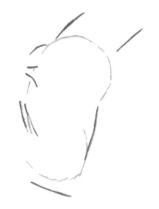
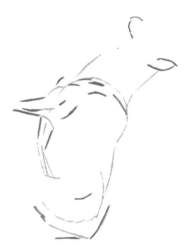

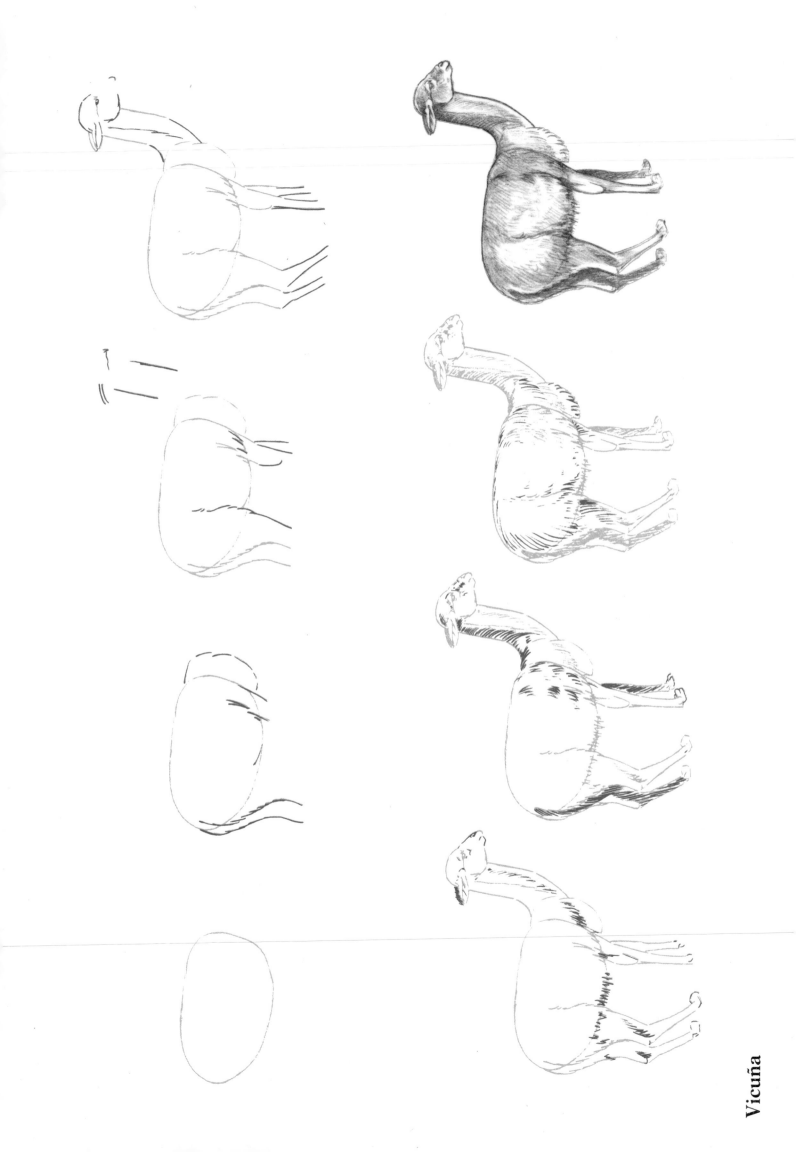

Vicuña

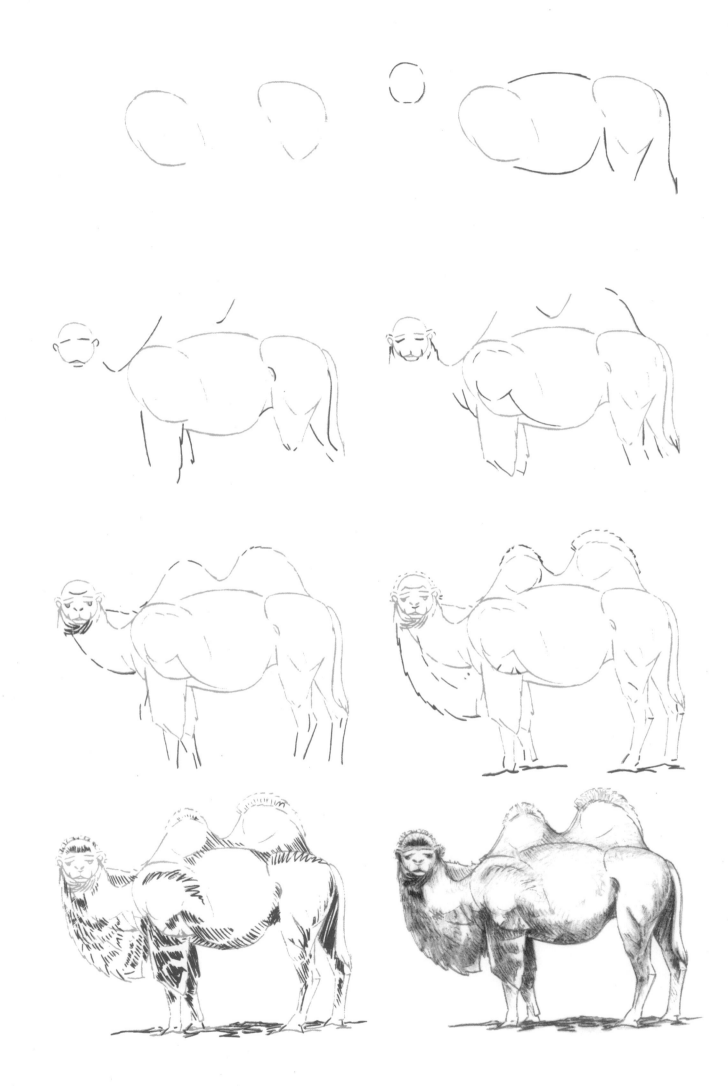

Bactrian Camel

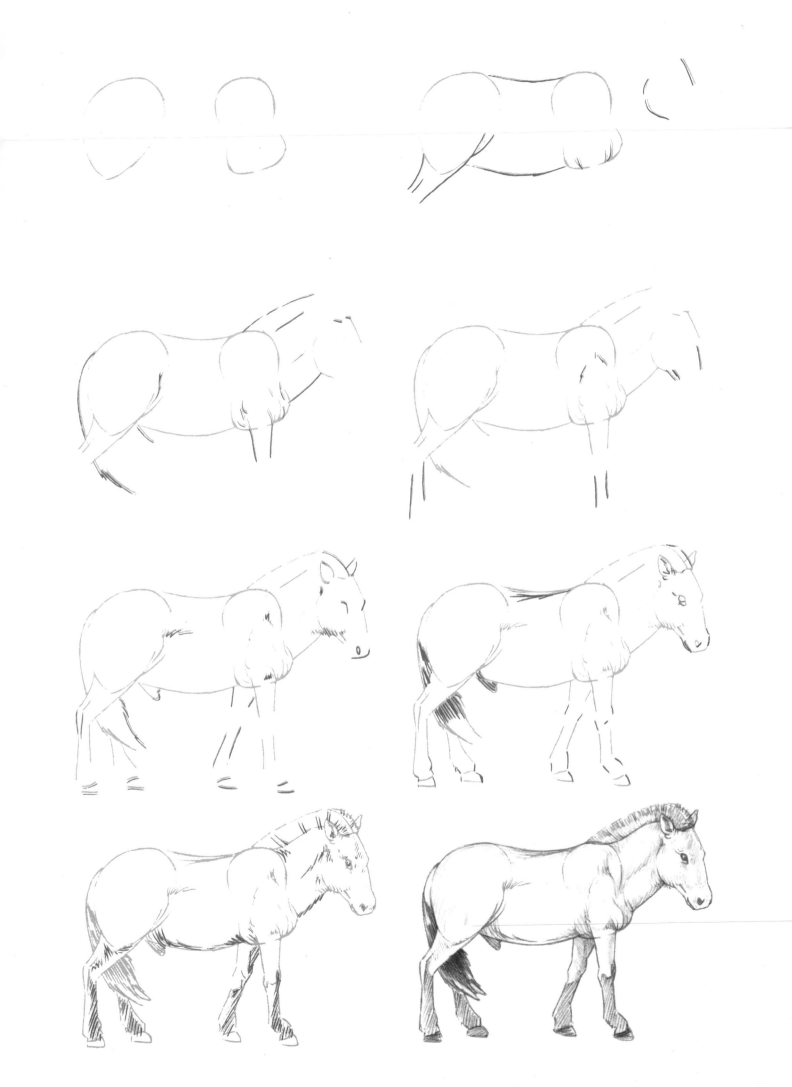

Przewalski's Horse

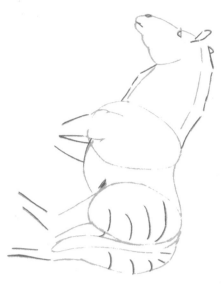
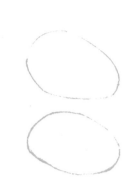

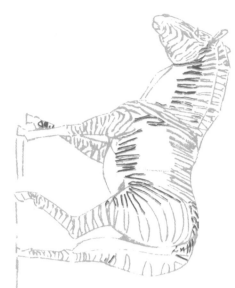
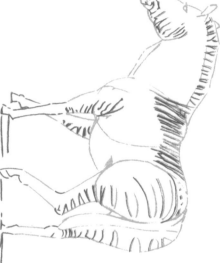
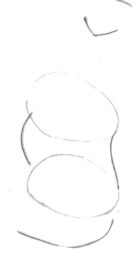

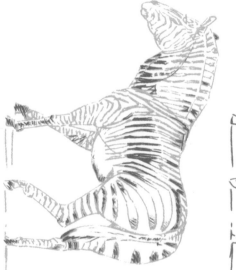
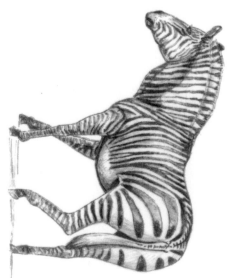
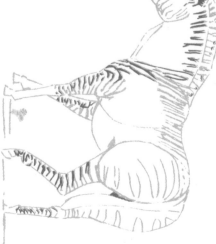
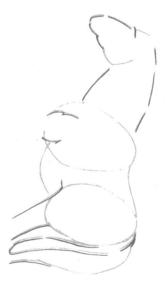

Mountain Zebra

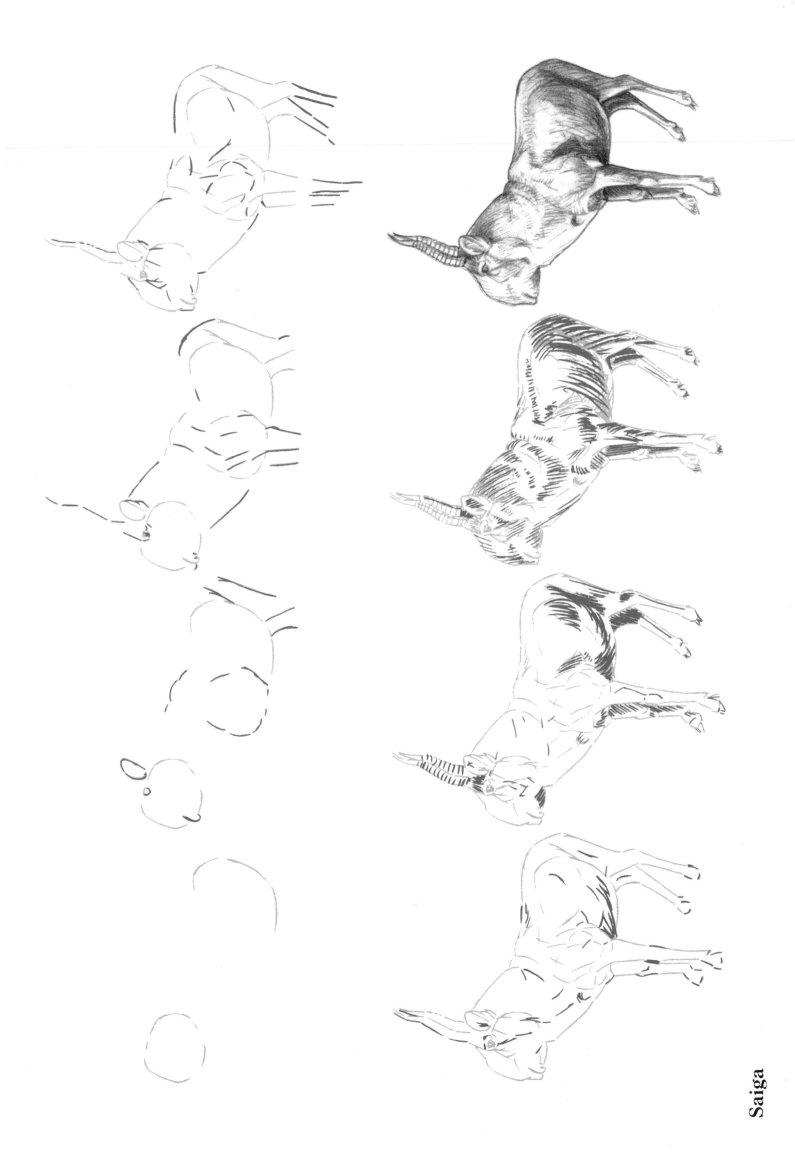

Saiga

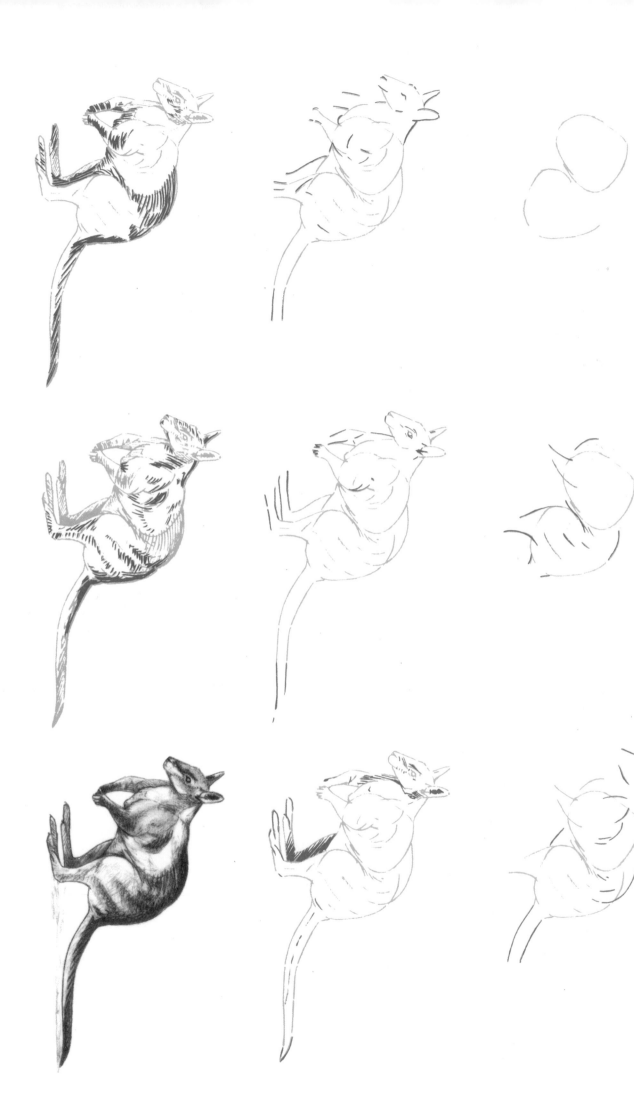

ABOUT THE AUTHOR

Lee J. Ames has been earning his living as an artist for almost forty years. He began his career working on Walt Disney's *Fantasia* and *Pinocchio*. He has taught at the School of Visual Arts in New York City and, more recently, at Dowling College on Long Island, New York State. He was, for a time, director of his own advertising agency and illustrator for several magazines. Mr Ames has illustrated over one hundred books, from preschool picture books to postgraduate texts. When not working, he battles on the tennis court. A native New Yorker, Lee J. Ames lives in Dix Hills, Long Island, with his wife, Jocelyn, their three dogs, and a calico cat.

Warren Budd has a bachelor's degree in fine arts. Primarily a natural science artist, he has been illustrating books for the past eight years. He lives in Long Island with his wife and two children.